THE CREATIVE

Vegetarian

COOKBOOK

THE CREATIVE

Vegetarian

COOKBOOK

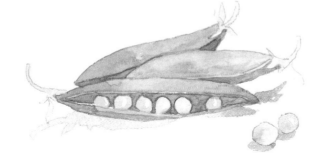

CLB

Colour Library Books

Watercolour paintings by Sally Brewer
Designed by Stonecastle Graphics
Edited by Jillian Stewart and Kate Cranshaw

CLB 4523
This edition published in 1996 by
Colour Library Books Ltd
Godalming Business Centre
Woolsack Way, Godalming, Surrey GU7 1XW
Tel: 01483 426266
© 1996 Colour Library Books Ltd
All rights reserved
ISBN 1-85833-510-8
Colour origination by Advance Laser Graphic Arts, Hong Kong
Printed and bound in Singapore by Tien Wah Press

Contents

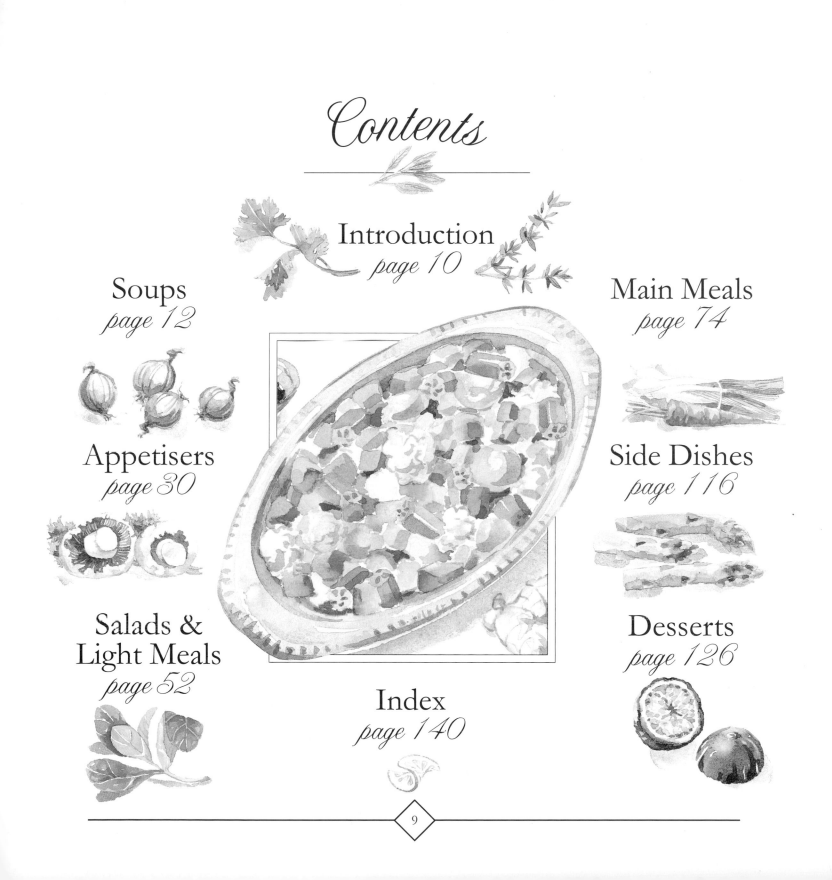

9

Introduction

Choosing to avoid eating meat is no longer a cranky thing to do. Every year thousands of people decide to cut out the meat, fish and fowl from their diet and turn vegetarian. No longer are vegetarians made to feel like freaks; their needs are becoming increasingly well catered for by food manufacturers, and even restaurants are now offering imaginative vegetarian dishes on their menus. But what do you prepare for everyday meals or for those special occasions when guests are expected? Putting into practice the decision to become a vegetarian can be daunting – as can the announcement by a member in a family of confirmed carnivores to turn vegetarian.

First must come a basic understanding of what constitutes a healthy vegetarian diet. Cutting out meat products that are high in fat is a positively healthy step to take, but be careful that you don't just substitute equally fatty cheese and eggs in their place. Make the effort to introduce a wide range of plant foods, and remember the advice to include four or five portions of fresh fruit (or fruit juice) and vegetables in your diet each day.

While fruit and vegetables are nutritious foods they do not contain significant amounts of protein. That is left to the plant protein foods. Cereal grains and their products such as oats, wheat (and flour, pasta and bulgar and couscous) rice, buckwheat, corn and millet, beans, dried peas and lentils, nuts and seeds as well as soya products such as tofu and TVP are all suitable foods for building the protein content of the diet. Do remember, however, that plant protein foods such as these contain a lower quality protein than animal foods. This deficiency can easily be overcome by serving different types of protein together – a grain and a bean product, a nut and bean or grain – or by mixing a plant protein with a dairy product which will contain a higher quality protein in itself. This is never as complex as it seems – consider a cheese sandwich, baked beans on toast, or lasagne; all mix different forms of vegetarian proteins to give a perfect balance.

Research monitoring the health of vegetarians suggests that their diet is typically lower in fat than that of the average person, and that this has a beneficial effect on health. Cutting out meat and meat products in particular is an obvious way of reducing fat intake, particularly the intake of the less desirable saturated fat. A vegetarian diet that depends too much on dairy foods, however, would not necessarily be any lower in saturated fat, so do try to include more of the lower-fat plant proteins.

A third aspect of balancing the diet is the fibre content. Ensuring there is sufficient fibre is important in maintaining a healthy digestive system. Whereas animal foods are devoid of fibre, all plant foods contain some fibre, with pulses (beans, peas and lentils) and wholewheat and oats especially rich. After the fibre, fat and protein elements of the diet come the vitamins and minerals. Vitamins are vital for proper body functioning; with each vitamin performing a specific task. Vitamin C is only found in fresh fruits and vegetables, so ensuring a good daily intake of these foods is the basis of a good vitamin C supply. The B group of vitamins is found in cereals and nuts and in small amounts in a wide range of dairy and plant foods with the exception of vitamin B12.

Vitamin B12 is found only in animal products – although small amounts have been traced in fermented soya products such as miso and in some seaweed. Generally, though, it is assumed that vegetarians eating dairy foods will rely on cheese, eggs and milk for their supply of vitamin B12, whereas vegans and others restricting dairy foods will need to include a fortified food;  yeast extract, some breakfast cereals and soya foods, as well as foods specifically for vegans, are all likely to have this crucial vitamin added, so check labels.

The other vitamin that might pose a problem for vegetarians is vitamin D. We traditionally derive a large amount of vitamin D from fish and fish liver oils, but this vitamin is also found in certain dairy foods and is added to margarine and some milk products.

Unlike other vitamins we are also able to manufacture our own supply by the action of the sun on the skin. Ensuring regular outdoor exercise and fresh air will boost vitamin D levels, but the housebound and young people may be in extra need of this vitamin.

Finally on the nutritional side are minerals, which like vitamins are required in only small amounts but which play a crucial role in health maintenace. The most significant mineral for vegetarians is iron, which is found in richest concentrations in meat and offal. Women of childbearing age and teenage girls in particular are most at risk from anaemia caused by a shortage of iron in the diet, so those following a vegetarian diet are further at risk. Ensure there is plenty of the following in the diet: leafy green vegetables such as spinach and watercress, wholegrain cereals, wheatgerm, eggs, nuts and dried apricots.

Following these simple nutritional steps will help to build the basis of a healthy vegetarian diet – now for the cooking!

Soups

Gone are the days when a soup without meat meant mixed vegetable! Today just about any vegetable can take centre stage in an exciting soup recipe all its own. Soups make good use of all manner of fresh produce, combining everyday or more exotic vegetables with herbs and spices or basic storecupboard standbys into a wealth of differently styled dishes.

Soup can take the form of a light first course dish, a perfect prelude to a formal dinner, or at the other end of the scale, served with a hunk of bread, it can make a hearty, filling meal in itself. In between lies a range of soups that are ideal for a light midday or evening snack. Whatever the soup, most can be conveniently prepared in advance and simply reheated when required.

Traditionally, soup has been regarded as a seasonal dish reserved for cold winter days. But just as salad can be enjoyed throughout the year, so have soups become the norm for all seasons.

Turning the traditional on its head are light, chilled soups, perfect for summer days or evenings. The classic Vichysoisse (p.14), a creamy blend of leek and potato, is one such dish that tastes good hot, but purists would argue should always be served cold.

Recipes designed to be served chilled should be just that – not lukewarm, but allowed to cool thoroughly and then seasoned to taste before serving. The flavour of a good soup comes from careful seasoning, appropriate use of herbs and spices, but more importantly from a good stock. Rarely do soup recipes call simply for water; nearly all require stock to give a really good flavour base. Making vegetable stock at home is much easier and less time consuming than the laborious meat-based stocks. For 2 pints (1.1 litres) stock, sauté a chopped onion in a little oil, stir in a chopped carrot, small turnip and four chopped celery sticks with a few cabbage leaves or celery tops. Pour over 3 pints (1.7 litres) cold water, bring to the boil, then simmer gently for 1-1^1/$_2$ hours, before straining. This stock will keep fresh for up to 48 hours in the fridge.

If time is tight, use a commercial stock cube or concentrate instead. There are several good vegetarian stock products on the market, so do experiment.

Home-made stock and most soups freeze well – but remember not to freeze recipes made with egg, cream or yogurt as they might separate out and the texture spoil. When it comes to serving soup don't forget to garnish carefully and to serve with bread, the fresher the better, the time honoured and still perfect accompaniment.

Cream of Cucumber —with Mint—

This delicious summer soup can be eaten hot, or chilled and served on ice for a refreshing change.

SERVES 4

3 large cucumbers
1 litre/1¾ pints vegetable stock
Salt and freshly ground black pepper
2-3 sprigs fresh mint
280ml/½ pint single cream
60ml/4 tbsps natural yogurt, to garnish

Cut one of the cucumbers in half and chop one half into small dice. Set the small dice to one side. Peel the remaining half and the other 2 cucumbers and roughly chop them into small pieces. Put the peeled cucumber, stock and seasoning into a large saucepan. Remove the mint leaves from the sprig and add the stalks only to the pan. Bring gently to the boil, reduce the heat and simmer gently for 25 minutes or until cucumber is tender.

Remove the mint stalks from the soup and, using a liquidiser or food processor, purée the soup until smooth. Return to the rinsed out pan and stir in the single cream and reserved diced cucumber. Reheat gently for about 5 minutes. To serve, finely chop the mint leaves and add to the soup. Stir a spoonful of yogurt into each bowl before serving.

Time: Preparation takes about 15 minutes, cooking takes about about 30 minutes.

Variation: Use a mixture of half stock and half pale ale for an interesting variation.

Vichyssoise

This classic French soup is both simple and economical to make.

SERVES 4

3 large leeks
45g/1½oz butter or margarine
2-3 medium potatoes, peeled and sliced
850ml/1½ pints vegetable stock
140ml/¼ pint milk
Salt and freshly ground black pepper
3 tbsps soured cream
Snipped chives, to garnish

Wash and trim the leeks, discarding the green parts. Slice the white part of the leeks thinly. Melt the butter or margarine in a large pan and sauté the leeks and potatoes for 10 minutes, stirring frequently until just softened. Add the stock and bring gently to the boil. Reduce heat and simmer for 30 minutes. Allow to cool slightly, pour the soup into a liquidiser or food processor and blend until smooth.

Return soup to the rinsed out pan. Stir in the milk, season and bring gently to simmering point. Chill before serving. Garnish with soured cream and snipped chives.

Time: Preparation takes about 15 minutes, cooking takes about 45 minutes.

Serving Idea: Vichyssoise is traditionally served chilled, but serve this soup hot for a delicious change.

Garden Vegetable Soup

A hearty soup perfect for those cold winter nights.

SERVES 4-6

1 tbsp butter or margarine
½ head fennel, finely chopped
3 medium carrots, diced
1 medium onion, chopped
2-3 cloves garlic, crushed
1 parsnip, diced
Salt and freshly ground black pepper
2 heaped tsps dried parsley
1 tbsp tomato purée
1 large potato, diced
1.14 litres/2 pints vegetable stock
60g/2oz frozen peas

Melt the margarine in a large pan and add the fennel, carrots, onion, garlic, parsnip and seasoning. Cover and allow to 'sweat' over a very low heat for 10-15 minutes, stirring occasionally. Add the parsley, tomato purée, potato and stock. Stir well, bring to the boil and simmer for 20-30 minutes, until the vegetables are tender.

Just before serving, add the frozen peas. Bring back to the boil and serve immediately.

Time: Preparation takes 15 minutes, cooking takes about 35 minutes.

Serving Idea: Serve with crusty rolls or French bread.

Spinach and Apple Soup

Two main flavours complement each other perfectly in this hearty soup.

SERVES 4

30g/1oz butter or margarine
1 small onion, chopped
30g/1oz wholemeal flour
570ml/1 pint vegetable stock
450g/1lb spinach, shredded
225g/8oz apple purée
280ml/½ pint milk
Salt and freshly ground black pepper
Pinch of nutmeg
Lemon juice
Natural yogurt
A little parsley, finely chopped

Melt the butter in a large saucepan and fry the onion until soft. Add the flour and cook to a roux. Add the stock slowly, stir well and simmer for 10 minutes. Add the spinach and cook until tender. Cool slightly and mix in the apple purée.

Place all the ingredients in a liquidiser and blend until smooth. Return to the pan and reheat slowly together with the milk. Add the salt, pepper, nutmeg and lemon juice to taste. Serve in individual bowls with the yogurt swirled on the top and garnished with chopped parsley.

Time: Preparation takes 15 minutes, cooking takes 15 minutes.

Cook's Tip: The apple purée can be omitted if not available, but it adds an unusual flavour to the soup.

Sweet Potato Soup

Warm up your winter nights with this heartening soup.

SERVES 4-6

60g/2oz butter or margarine
1 large onion, finely chopped
450g/1lb sweet potatoes, peeled and diced
225g/8oz carrots, peeled and diced
1 tbsp chopped coriander
Grated rind and juice of 1 lemon
850ml/1½ pints vegetable stock
Freshly ground black pepper

Melt the butter or margarine and cook the onion until transparent. Add the sweet potato and carrots and allow to 'sweat' over a very low heat for 10-15 minutes, stirring occasionally. Add the coriander, lemon zest, juice of half the lemon, stock and pepper. Cover and simmer for 30-40 minutes. Liquidise until almost smooth, leaving some texture to the soup. Return to the pan and reheat until piping hot. Garnish with coriander leaves and serve immediately.

Time: Preparation takes 15 minutes, cooking takes 40-55 minutes.
Serving Idea: Serve with granary rolls.
Cook's Tip: Fresh coriander may be kept in a jug of water in a cool place. It can also be frozen for use when fresh is not available.

Easy Lentil Soup

A good old-fashioned soup which is sure to please all the family.

SERVES 4-6

225g/8oz split red lentils
30g/1oz butter or margarine
1 medium onion, finely chopped
2 stalks celery, finely diced
2 carrots, scrubbed and finely diced
Grated rind of 1 lemon
1.14 litres/2 pints light vegetable stock
Salt and freshly ground black pepper

Pick over the lentils and remove any stones. Rinse well. Heat the butter or margarine in a pan and sauté the onion for 2-3 minutes. Add the diced celery and carrots and let the vegetables sweat for 5-10 minutes. Stir in the lentils, add the lemon rind, stock and salt and pepper to taste. Bring to the boil, reduce the heat and simmer for 15-20 minutes, until the vegetables are tender.

Roughly blend the soup in a liquidiser, it should not be too smooth. Adjust the seasoning and reheat gently.

Time: Preparation takes about 10 minutes, cooking takes 15-20 minutes.
Serving Idea: Sprinkle with cheese and serve with hot toast.
Freezing: Freeze for up to 3 months.

Vegetable Soup

This hearty vegetable soup makes the most of traditional and unusual vegetables.

SERVES 4

2 tbsps vegetable oil
1 large carrot, peeled and diced
1 large turnip, peeled and diced
2 leeks, washed and thinly sliced
2 potatoes, scrubbed and diced
570ml/1 pint vegetable stock
450g/1lb can plum tomatoes, chopped
1 bay leaf
¼ tsp dried savory or marjoram
60g/2oz soup pasta
Salt and freshly ground black pepper
90g/3oz fresh or frozen sliced green beans
120g/4oz okra, trimmed and sliced
60g/2oz frozen sweetcorn niblets
60g/2oz frozen peas
1 tbsp chopped parsley

Heat the oil in a large saucepan and add the carrot, turnip, leeks and potatoes. Sauté gently for about 10 minutes or until softened. Stir in the stock, tomatoes, bay leaf, savory or marjoram, soup pasta, salt and pepper. Bring gently to the boil, reduce the heat and simmer gently for 20 minutes.

Add the beans and okra and cook for a further 10 minutes. Finally add the sweetcorn, peas and parsley. Cook for 5 minutes before serving.

Time: Preparation takes about 20 minutes, cooking takes about 45 minutes.

Cook's Tip: This recipe can be adapted for vegans by omitting the soup pasta and replacing it with brown rice.

Variation: Use any combination of vegetables in season to vary this soup.

Preparation: If tinned tomatoes are not available, add 340g/12oz fresh tomatoes and 140ml/¼ pint vegetable stock or water instead.

Salad Soup

A delicious, unusual soup that is as refreshing as its
name implies.

SERVES 4-6

2-3 medium potatoes, peeled and diced
420ml/³/₄ pint vegetable stock
6 spring onions, finely chopped
¹/₂ head lettuce, washed and shredded
120g/4oz fresh spinach leaves, washed, trimmed and shredded
1 bunch watercress, washed, trimmed and chopped
¹/₂ cucumber, peeled and grated or diced
570ml/1 pint milk
2 tbsps chopped fresh parsley
Pinch of nutmeg
Pinch of cayenne pepper
Salt and freshly ground black pepper
140ml/¹/₄ pint single cream
Natural yogurt and slices of cucumber, to garnish

Cook the potatoes in the stock for 15 minutes or until tender. Add all the remaining vegetables and cook for a further 5 minutes. Pour into a liquidiser or food processor and purée until smooth. Return to the rinsed out pan.

Stir in the milk and parsley and season with nutmeg, cayenne pepper, salt and pepper. Add the cream and reheat gently, but do not allow to boil. Garnish with swirls of natural yogurt and slices of cucumber before serving.

Time: Preparation takes about 10 minutes, cooking takes about 25 minutes.

Green Pea Soup

Pale green and creamy, this delicious soup is made with
frozen peas, making it possible to enjoy the taste of summer
all year round.

SERVES 4

30g/1oz butter or margarine
1 shallot, finely chopped
30g/1oz plain flour
280ml/¹/₂ pint vegetable stock
420ml/³/₄ pint milk
450g/1lb frozen peas
¹/₄ tsp dried marjoram
1 tbsp chopped fresh parsley
Salt and freshly ground black pepper
1 small bunch fresh mint
140ml/¹/₄ pint single cream

Melt the butter or margarine in a saucepan and sauté the shallot until soft. Stir in the flour and cook gently for about 1 minute. Remove the pan from the heat and gradually add the stock and milk. Reserve about 90g/3oz of the peas and add the rest to the pan, along with the marjoram, parsley and seasoning. Heat gently until thickened slightly. Pour the soup into a liquidiser or food processor and purée until smooth.

Using a sharp knife, chop the mint very finely. Stir the mint along with the cream into the puréed soup. Stir in the reserved peas and reheat gently before serving.

Time: Preparation takes about 10 minutes, cooking takes about 15 minutes.

Tomato and Dill Bisque

This sophisticated soup, with its delicate flavour, is an elegant starter to serve at a summer lunch or dinner.

SERVES 4

900g/2lbs fresh tomatoes

1 tbsp vegetable oil

1 onion, chopped

2 large sprigs fresh dill

2 tbsps tomato purée

Salt and freshly ground black pepper

850ml/1½ pints vegetable stock

140ml/¼ pint double cream

2 tsps chopped fresh dill

60ml/4 tbsps natural yogurt

4 slices fresh tomato

4 small sprigs fresh dill

Cut the tomatoes in half over a bowl and remove and discard the seeds, reserving any juice that is produced. Heat the oil in a saucepan and sauté the onion until softened. Add the tomato flesh, tomato juice, dill sprigs, tomato purée, salt, pepper and stock. Bring gently to the boil and simmer for 10 minutes.

Remove the sprigs of dill and, using a liquidiser or food processor, purée the soup until smooth. Strain the puréed soup back into the pan through a sieve to remove the skins. Stir in the double cream and chopped dill, and reheat gently, stirring constantly. Do not allow to boil at this point. Garnish each serving with a spoonful of the yogurt, a tomato slice and a sprig of dill.

Time: Preparation takes about 20 minutes, cooking takes about 20 minutes.

Parsnip & Carrot Soup

A delicious and wholesome country soup which makes good use of that favourite vegetable, the humble parsnip.

SERVES 4

225g/8oz parsnips, peeled and sliced
225g/8oz carrots, peeled and sliced
280ml/½ pint vegetable stock
570ml/1 pint milk
Salt and freshly ground black pepper
Pinch of ground nutmeg
1 small bunch chives, snipped
60ml/4 tbsps single cream

Cook the parsnips and carrots in the stock for about 15 minutes until tender. Place in a liquidiser or food processor and purée until smooth. Return to the rinsed out pan. Add the milk, season with salt, pepper and nutmeg, and stir in the chives. Reheat gently until just simmering. Stir in the cream and serve.

Time: Preparation takes about 10 minutes, cooking takes about 20 minutes.

Serving Idea: Serve with crisp French bread and a vegetarian cheese.

Freezing: This soup will keep for up to 3 months if frozen before the final addition of the cream. This can be added just before serving.

Preparation: If a very smooth soup is required, the puréed soup can be strained through a metal sieve before the chives are added.

Cheddar Cheese Soup

An unusual soup that is ideal for using up any leftover cheese.

SERVES 4

225g/8oz vegetarian Cheddar cheese
45g/1½oz butter or margarine
1 carrot, peeled and diced
2 sticks celery, trimmed and chopped
30g/1oz plain flour
420ml/¾ pint vegetable stock
570ml/1 pint milk
1 bay leaf
¼ tsp dried thyme
Chopped parsley, to garnish

Grate the cheese finely and, if using more than one type, mix together. Melt the butter or margarine in a pan and sauté the carrot and celery until just soft. Stir in the flour and cook for about 30 seconds. Remove from the heat and gradually add the stock and milk. Add the bay leaf and thyme. Return to the heat and cook gently until thickened slightly, stirring constantly.

Add the cheese a little at a time, stirring until it has melted. Remove the bay leaf and serve the soup sprinkled with chopped parsley.

Time: Preparation takes about 10 minutes, cooking takes about 20 minutes.

Serving Idea: Serve with caraway or rye bread.

Sherry Cream Soup with ─ Walnuts ─

This unusual soup is hearty and filling; ideal for a cold day.

SERVES 4

900g/2lbs mushrooms, trimmed and chopped
5-6 slices stale bread, crusts removed
700ml/1¼ pints vegetable stock
1 sprig of fresh thyme
1 bay leaf
½ clove garlic, crushed
Salt and freshly ground black pepper
420ml/¾ pint single cream
60ml/4 tbsps sherry
140ml/¼ pint whipped cream
Grated nutmeg, to garnish

Place the mushrooms in a large pan and crumble the bread over them. Add the stock, thyme, bay leaf, garlic, salt and pepper. Bring to the boil, reduce the heat and simmer gently for 20 minutes, or until mushrooms are soft, stirring occasionally.

Remove the bay leaf and thyme. Using a liquidiser or food processor, blend the soup until a smooth purée is formed. Return to the rinsed out pan. Whisk in the single cream and sherry. Reheat gently but do not allow to boil. Garnish each serving of soup with a spoonful of the whipped cream and a sprinkling of nutmeg.
Time: Preparation takes about 20 minutes, cooking takes about 25 minutes.

Purée of Asparagus ─ Soup ─

This thick and creamy soup makes full use of the delicate flavour of fresh summer asparagus.

SERVES 4

1.4kg/3lbs asparagus, fresh or frozen and thawed
1 litre/1¾ pints vegetable stock
¼ tsp ground mace
Salt and freshly ground black pepper
280ml/½ pint single cream
140ml/¼ pint whipped cream
Sprinkling of ground mace

Trim the thick ends from the asparagus and cut away any tough outer skin. Chop the spears into 2.5cm/1-inch pieces. Bring the stock to the boil in a large pan, add the asparagus, mace and seasoning, and cook for about 10 minutes or until asparagus is just tender.

Using a liquidiser or food processor, blend the asparagus in the cooking liquid until it becomes a smooth purée. Return the asparagus to the rinsed out pan and stir in the single cream. Reheat gently but do not allow to boil or the cream will curdle. Garnish each serving with a spoonful of the whipped cream and a dusting of the ground mace.
Time: Preparation takes about 15 minutes, cooking takes about about 15 minutes.
Serving Idea: Serve with slices of wholemeal bread for a luxurious first course.

Creamy Spinach Soup

The wonderful combination of spinach and cream in this soup could not fail to please even the most fussy guest.

SERVES 4-6

900g/2lbs fresh spinach, trimmed and well washed
30g/1oz butter or margarine
1 shallot, finely chopped
30g/1oz plain flour
700ml/1¼ pints vegetable stock
¼ tsp dried marjoram
1 bay leaf
Pinch of grated nutmeg
Salt and freshly ground black pepper
Squeeze of lemon juice
420ml/¾ pint milk
140ml/¼ pint single cream
Slices of lemon or chopped hard-boiled egg, to garnish

Cook the spinach until just wilted in a covered saucepan with just the water that is left clinging to the leaves. Melt the butter or margarine in a large pan and sauté the shallot until soft. Stir the flour into the pan and cook for about 30 seconds. Remove from the heat and gradually add the stock. Add the marjoram, bay leaf and nutmeg. Return to the heat and cook gently until thickened slightly, stirring constantly.

Remove the bay leaf and discard. Add the spinach to the pan. Season with salt and pepper and add the lemon juice. Purée the soup in a liquidiser or food processor until smooth. Return to the rinsed out pan and stir in the milk. Bring gently to simmering point. Stir in the cream just before serving. Serve garnished with lemon slices or chopped hard-boiled eggs.

Time: Preparation takes about 15 minutes, cooking takes about about 20 minutes.

Variation: Use a mixture of watercress and spinach for a tasty variation.

Serving Idea: Serve with crunchy wholemeal croutons.

Freezing: This soup will freeze successfully for up to 3 months without the cream and garnish.

Fennel and Walnut Soup

A delicious and unusual combination of ingredients makes this soup perfect for special occasions.

SERVES 4

1 bulb fennel, chopped

1 head celery, chopped

1 large onion, chopped

1 tbsp olive or sunflower oil

90g/3oz walnuts, crushed

1.14 litres/2 pints vegetable stock, bean stock or water

3 tbsps Pernod

140ml/¼ pint single cream

Salt and freshly ground black pepper

Parsley to garnish

Sauté the fennel, celery and onion in the oil over a low heat. Add the walnuts and stock and simmer for half an hour. Blend the simmered ingredients together and return to the pan. Add the Pernod, single cream and salt and pepper. Reheat gently and serve garnished with parsley.

Time: Preparation takes about 15 minutes, cooking about 1 hour 10 minutes.

Serving Idea: Celery leaves may be used as a garnish if no parsley is available.

Variation: Other nuts such as cashews or almonds may be used in place of walnuts.

Watchpoint: Do not allow the soup to boil after adding the cream and Pernod.

Miso Soup

This delicious soup of Japanese origin makes a nice change for a starter.

SERVES 2

1 small onion, grated

2.5cm/1-inch fresh root ginger, peeled and finely chopped

1 clove garlic, crushed

1 tsp sesame oil

1 carrot, peeled and finely sliced

¼ small cauliflower, divided into florets

1.14ml/2 pints water

1 large tbsp arame (Japanese seaweed)

30g/1oz peas (fresh or frozen)

2 tbsps shoyu (Japanese soy sauce)

1 tbsp miso (red bean paste)

Freshly ground black pepper to taste

2 spring onions, finely chopped

Sauté the onion, ginger and garlic in the sesame oil for a few minutes. Add the carrot and cauliflower and gently sweat the vegetables for 5 minutes. Add the water, arame, peas and shoyu. Cook for 15-20 minutes until the vegetables are soft. Blend the miso to a paste with a little of the soup liquid and add to the soup but do not allow to boil. Season with freshly ground black pepper to taste. Serve garnished with chopped spring onions.

Time: Preparation takes 15 minutes, cooking takes 20 minutes.

Serving Idea: Serve with hot garlic bread.

Cook's Tip: Arame, shoyu and miso are available from Japanese grocers.

Spring Vegetable Soup

Spring vegetables combine to produce a delightfully light soup with a glorious fresh flavour.

1 litre/1¾ pints vegetable stock
120g/4oz fresh shelled peas
3 carrots, peeled and cut into thin 5cm/2-inch strips
120g/4oz French beans, cut into 2.5cm/1-inch pieces
120g/4oz asparagus, cut into 2.5cm/1-inch pieces
1 head green cabbage, finely shredded
3 spring onions, sliced
1 red pepper, sliced
60ml/4 tbsps white wine (optional)
Salt and freshly ground black pepper

Bring the stock to the boil in a large pan, add the peas, simmer gently for 10 minutes, and then add the carrots and simmer for another 10 minutes. Stir in the beans, asparagus and cabbage and cook for 5 minutes. Finally add the spring onions, red pepper and white wine, if using. Cook for 5 minutes then season to taste before serving.

Time: Preparation takes about 25 minutes, cooking takes about about 30 minutes.

Preparation: Trim away the hard core of the cabbage and only use the finely shredded leaves in this recipe.

Serving Idea: Serve with crunchy French toast.

Cream of Carrot Soup

A classic soup which is suitable for any occasion.

SERVES 4

1 large onion, chopped
2 cloves garlic, crushed
1 tbsp olive oil
450g/1lb carrots, chopped
1 tsp mixed herbs
850ml/1½ pints stock
140ml/¼ pint soured cream
Salt and freshly ground black pepper

Sauté the chopped onion and garlic in the oil until transparent. Add the carrots, mixed herbs and stock. Bring to the boil and simmer for about 30 minutes, until the carrots are soft. Cool a little and then liquidise until smooth. Add the soured cream, season to taste and mix thoroughly. Heat through gently and serve.

Time: Preparation takes about 10 minutes, cooking takes 35 minutes.

Watchpoint: Do not allow the soup to boil after adding the soured cream.

Variation: For a richer soup, omit the soured cream and add a swirl of double cream just before serving.

Tomato and Leek Soup

This delicious combination of leeks and sweet tomatoes is sure to become a firm favourite.

SERVES 4-6

2 large leeks, washed, trimmed and finely sliced
570ml/1 pint fresh tomato juice
Dash of Tabasco or soy sauce
¼ tsp celery seasoning
Shake of garlic powder
4 fresh tomatoes, skinned and sliced
Salt and freshly ground black pepper

Cook the leeks in about 280ml/½ pint of boiling water for 15 minutes, or until tender. Remove about half the leeks from the cooking liquid and set aside. Purée the remaining leeks with the cooking liquid, in a liquidiser or food processor. Return the puréed leeks to the rinsed out pan and add another 280ml/½ pint water. Stir in the tomato juice, Tabasco or soy sauce, celery seasoning and garlic powder. Heat gently to simmering point then add the reserved leeks and tomato slices, and season with salt and pepper. Cook gently for 3-4 minutes and serve hot.
Time: Preparation takes about 10 minutes, cooking takes about about 20 minutes.
Serving Idea: Serve with crusty French bread and vegetarian Cheddar cheese.
Freezing: This soup will freeze for up to 6 weeks. Freeze in a rigid 2-litre/3-pint container.

Gazpacho

One of Spain's tastiest exports.

SERVES 4

450g/1lb ripe tomatoes
1 small onion
1 small green pepper
1 clove garlic, crushed
¼ medium cucumber
1 tbsp red wine vinegar
1 tbsp olive oil
400g/14oz can tomato juice
1-2 tbsps lime juice
Salt and freshly ground black pepper

Plunge the tomatoes into boiling water, leave for 2 minutes, then remove the skins and seeds. Chop the onion and pepper and place in a liquidiser with the tomatoes, garlic, cucumber, vinegar, oil and tomato juice. Purée until smooth. Add the lime juice and seasoning to taste. Pour the soup into a glass dish and chill until required.
Time: Preparation takes 10 minutes.
Serving Idea: Serve garnished with croutons and finely diced cucumber.
Watchpoint: If the soup is too thick, add more tomato juice after chilling.
Variation: Lemon juice may be used in place of the lime juice.

Wild Rice Soup

A meal in itself when served with granary bread and a green salad.

SERVES 4

60g/2oz wild rice

420ml/³/₄ pint water

2 onions, chopped

15g/¹/₂oz butter or ghee

2 sticks celery, chopped

¹/₂ tsp dried thyme

¹/₂ tsp dried sage

850ml/1¹/₂ pints water or vegetable stock

2 tsps Vecon (vegetable stock)

1 tbsp shoyu (Japanese soy sauce)

6 small potatoes, peeled and roughly chopped

1 carrot, finely diced

Milk or single cream

Add the wild rice to the water, bring to the boil, reduce the heat and simmer for 40-50 minutes, until the rice has puffed and most of the liquid has been absorbed.

Sauté the onions in the butter until transparent. Add the celery, thyme and sage and cook for 5-10 minutes. Add the water, Vecon, shoyu and potatoes. Simmer for 20 minutes, or until  the potatoes are cooked. Blend the mixture in a liquidiser until smooth. Return to the pan and add the carrot and wild rice. Add the milk or cream to thin the soup to the desired consistency. Reheat gently and serve.

Time: Preparation takes about 15 minutes. Cooking takes 30 minutes plus 40 minutes to cook the wild rice.

Cook's Tip: You can prepare and cook the soup whilst the wild rice is cooking. Add the rice to the soup at the end of the cooking time.

Freezing: Cook a large quantity of wild rice and freeze in small portions. Add to the soup or other dishes as needed.

Variation: Toast some flaked almonds and sprinkle on top of the soup before serving.

Split Pea Soup

A classic soup which looks extra special with a swirl of yogurt on top.

SERVES 6

225g/8oz split peas
1.7 litres/3 pints vegetable stock
60g/2oz butter or margarine
1 large onion, chopped
3 sticks celery, chopped
2 leeks, finely sliced
2 medium potatoes, peeled and diced
1 medium carrot, finely chopped
Salt and freshly ground black pepper

Cook the peas in the stock for 10-15 minutes. Meanwhile, melt the margarine and sauté the onion, celery and leeks for a few minutes. Add to the peas and stock together with the potatoes and carrot and bring back to the boil. Simmer for 30 minutes. Season well and liquidise until smooth.

Time: Preparation takes about 10 minutes, cooking takes 40 minutes.

Serving Idea: If the vegetables are chopped small enough you can serve this as a chunky soup.

Cook's Tip: If you do not have a liquidiser you can pass the soup through a sieve, although it will not be quite as thick.

French Onion Soup

This soup tastes best if cooked the day before it is needed and then reheated as required.

SERVES 4

3 medium onions
60g/2oz butter or margarine
30g/1oz plain flour or soya flour
1 litre/1¼ pints boiling vegetable stock
Salt and freshly ground black pepper

Topping

4 slices French bread, cut crosswise
60g/2oz vegetarian Cheddar cheese, grated
30g/1oz vegetarian Parmesan cheese, grated

Slice the onions very finely into rings. Melt the butter in a pan, add the onion rings and fry over a medium heat until well browned. Mix in the flour and stir well until browned. Add the stock and seasoning and simmer for 30 minutes.

Toast the bread on both sides. Combine the cheeses, and divide between the bread slices; grill until golden brown. Place the slices of bread and cheese in the bottom of individual soup dishes and spoon the soup over the top. Serve at once.

Time: Preparation takes 10 minutes, cooking takes 30 minutes.

Variation: For a special occasion, add a tablespoonful of brandy to the stock.

Watchpoint: The onions must be very well browned, as it is this which gives the soup its rich colour.

Chestnut Soup

This unusual soup is high in protein and dietary fibre, and is so delicious that it will become a firm family favourite.

SERVES 4

30g/1oz butter or margarine
2 sticks of celery, trimmed and finely chopped
2 large onions, chopped
225g/8oz unsweetened chestnut purée
850ml/1½ pints home-made vegetable stock
Salt and freshly ground black pepper
Wholemeal croutons, to garnish

Melt the butter or margarine in a large saucepan and sauté the celery and onion until just soft. Blend the chestnut purée with a little of the stock and add to the pan along with the remaining stock. Season with salt and pepper. Bring gently to the boil, reduce the heat and simmer gently for 35 minutes. Serve garnished with the croutons.

Time: Preparation takes about 15 minutes and cooking takes about 40 minutes.

Preparation: If unsweetened chestnut purée is unavailable, cook 225g/8oz shelled chestnuts in 140ml/¼ pint boiling water until they are soft, and purée these in a liquidiser or food processor.

Freezing: This soup will freeze for 1 month.

Beetroot & Sour Cream Soup

This delicious and unusual soup is worthy of any occasion.

450g/1lb fresh beetroot
225g/8oz turnips, peeled and cut into even-sized pieces
1 litre/1¾ pints vegetable stock
1 bay leaf
Salt and freshly ground black pepper
280ml/½ pint soured cream
1 tbsp grated fresh or bottled horseradish
Snipped chives, to garnish

Boil the beetroot in salted water for about 30-40 minutes or until soft. (Large older beetroot may take longer.) Remove from the pan and leave until cold enough to handle. Carefully remove the skins and any roots from the cooked beetroots using a small knife. Cut the cooked beetroot into small pieces and put these, along with the turnips, stock, bay leaf, salt and pepper, into a large saucepan. Bring to the boil, then reduce the heat and simmer gently for 20 minutes or until the turnip is tender. Remove the bay leaf and discard.

Using a liquidiser or food processor, blend the soup until it becomes a smooth purée. Return to the rinsed out pan. Reserve 60ml/4 tbsps of the soured cream and stir the remainder into the soup along with the horseradish.

Reheat gently for a few minutes but do not allow the soup to boil. Serve the soup topped with the reserved cream and a sprinkling of snipped chives.

Time: Preparation takes about 20 minutes, cooking takes about 1 hour.

Freezing: This soup will freeze for up to 2 months.

Sweetcorn & Red Pepper Soup

This creamy soup has a definite bite to its flavour and can be made with either fresh or canned sweetcorn kernels.

SERVES 4

4 medium potatoes, scrubbed and cut into even-sized pieces
1 bay leaf
570ml/1 pint vegetable stock
15g/¹⁄₂oz butter or margarine
1 onion, chopped
1 large red pepper, deseeded and chopped
1 red chilli, chopped
225g/8oz sweetcorn kernels
570ml/1 pint milk
Salt and freshly ground black pepper
Freshly chopped parsley, to garnish

Place the potatoes in a saucepan with the bay leaf and cover with the stock. Bring to the boil and simmer gently for 15 minutes or until tender. Remove the bay leaf, then pour the potatoes and stock into a liquidiser or food processor and blend until smooth.

Melt the butter or margarine in another pan and add the onion, red pepper and chilli. Sauté gently for 5-10 minutes or until soft. Add the puréed potatoes to the pan along with the sweetcorn and milk, stir to blend thoroughly. Reheat gently and season to taste. Serve garnished with chopped parsley.

Variation: If preparing this soup for vegans, substitute soya milk for fresh milk, but do not boil the soup after this addition, and use non-dairy margarine.

Time: Preparation takes about 20 minutes, cooking takes about about 30 minutes.

Serving Idea: Serve with fresh, crusty rolls.

Cook's Tip: Great care must be taken when preparing fresh chillies. Use clean rubber gloves and do not get the juice near eyes or mouth. Rinse eyes with lots of clear cold water should you accidently get juice in them.

Appetisers

Newcomers to vegetarian cookery, faced with the prospect of preparing a three-course meal, might well fall at the first hurdle! Finding a suitable first course recipe for a dinner party can seem a problem, but in practice there are plenty of ingredients that can be transformed into tempting appetisers to get any meal off to a good start.

Pâtés might well have unacceptable connotations, but surprisingly good pâtés can be prepared from a base of vegetables, with creamy tofu, beans or even nuts adding extra body. The classic hummus, made from puréed, cooked chickpeas is one starter acceptable to all, vegetarian or not. Hummus (p. 51) and other simple dipping textured pâtés and spreads make informal appetisers, perfect for serving with crudités of raw vegetables or dainty squares of melba toast or strips of pitta bread.

Attractively arranged salads also make a good choice for a first course. Adding unusual ingredients to the more familiar salads will give an unexpected twist, while for a really impressive result try to serve them with a home-made dressing. Arrange on the plate just before serving for maximum freshness.

Many first course favourites are served cold, but there is no reason why even elements of a salad couldn't be hot – just watch out for overcooking. Freshness and maximum visual appeal underlie the success of a starter to set the tone for a meal. Dishes requiring a minimum of cooking are ideal – just a brief heating time to ensure that the cook doesn't spend too long in the kitchen.

For vegetarian cooks, small vegetables can make perfect centrepieces for starters. Although stuffed mushrooms are something of a cliché, peppers, aubergines, artichokes and tomatoes all make excellent subjects for savoury stuffing mixtures.

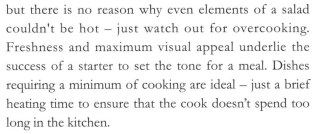

Choose dishes with an exciting spiciness or strong flavour to really whet the appetite. It's no wonder that garlic features so frequently in favourite starter recipes. Its wonderful aroma easily escapes from the kitchen to entice and encourage digestive juices to be set flowing. By the time garlic mushrooms or garlic bread hit the table, guests are more than ready to tuck in.

First courses should never be too enticing though – there's nothing more frustrating than to reach the second course of the meal only to find everyone's appetite has been satiated by the starter. Better to serve fair-sized portions, without appearing mean; smaller plates help make a little appear more, and particularly hungry eaters can always fill up with extra bread if they really can't wait for more!

Watercress & Mushroom Pâté

A delightful pâté which is perfect garnished with lime or lemon wedges and served with thinly sliced brown bread and butter.

SERVES 4

30g/1oz butter or margarine
1 medium onion, finely chopped
90g/3oz dark, flat mushrooms, finely chopped
1 bunch watercress, finely chopped
120g/4oz low fat curd cheese
Few drops of shoyu sauce (Japanese soy sauce)
Scant ½ tsp caraway seeds
Freshly ground black pepper

Melt the butter over a low heat and cook the onion until soft but not coloured. Raise the heat, add the mushrooms and cook quickly for 2 minutes. Add the chopped watercress and stir for about 30 seconds, until it becomes limp.

Place the contents of the pan in a blender together with the cheese and shoyu sauce. Blend until smooth. Stir in the caraway seeds and pepper to taste. Put into individual ramekin dishes or one large serving dish and chill for at least 2 hours until firm.

Time: Preparation takes 10 minutes, cooking takes 5 minutes.

Cook's Tip: It may be necessary to stir the contents of the blender several times as the mixture should be fairly thick.

Flageolet Fiesta

Serve this dish on its own as a starter or as a snack with lots of crusty bread.

SERVES 4

225g/8oz flageolet beans, soaked overnight
1 medium onion
1 clove garlic
Half a cucumber
2 tbsps chopped parsley
2 tbsps chopped mint
2 tbsps olive oil
Grated rind and juice of 1 lemon
Salt and freshly ground black pepper
Watercress to garnish

Cook the flageolet beans in plenty of boiling water for about 1 hour or until just tender. Drain and put into a mixing bowl. Peel and finely chop the onion. Crush the garlic and chop the cucumber into bite-sized pieces. Add the onion, garlic, cucumber, herbs, oil, lemon juice and rind to the beans and mix well. Add seasoning to taste and leave to marinate  for 2 hours. Transfer to a clean serving bowl. Serve garnished with watercress.

Time: Preparation takes 15 minutes. Marinating takes 2 hours and cooking takes 1 hour.

Variation: Substitute red kidney beans for flageolet beans.

Indonesian-Style Stuffed — Peppers —

For this adaptable recipe you can substitute pine nuts or peanuts if you don't have cashews.

SERVES 8

2 tbsps olive oil

1 medium onion, chopped

1 clove garlic, crushed

2 tsps turmeric

1 tsp crushed coriander seed

2 tbsps desiccated coconut

120g/4oz mushrooms, chopped

90g/3oz bulgar wheat

60g/2oz raisins

30g/1oz creamed coconut

280ml/½ pint stock or water

200g/7oz tomatoes, skinned and chopped

60g/2oz cashew nuts

4 small green peppers, cut in half lengthways

2 tsps lemon juice

Stock for cooking

Heat the oil and fry the onion and garlic until lightly browned. Add the turmeric, coriander and desiccated coconut and cook gently for about 2 minutes. Add the mushrooms and bulgar wheat and cook for a further 2 minutes. Add the rest of the ingredients except the nuts, lemon juice, peppers and stock, and simmer gently for 15-20 minutes until the bulgar wheat is cooked.

Toast the cashew nuts in a dry frying pan until golden brown. Blanch the peppers in boiling water for 3 minutes. Mix the nuts and lemon juice with the rest of the ingredients (except the stock) and fill the peppers with the mixture. Place the filled peppers in a large casserole dish and pour stock around the peppers. Bake in an oven preheated to 180°C/350°F/Gas Mark 4, for 20 minutes. Drain peppers and place on a hot plate to serve.
Time: Preparation takes 20 minutes, cooking takes 45 minutes.
Freezing: The cooked peppers will freeze well for up to 3 months.

Tomato Chartreuse

This delicately flavoured starter is ideal for a warm summer's day.

SERVES 4

2-3 tbsps agar-agar
Juice of ½ lemon
340ml/12fl oz tomato juice
2 tsps tomato purée
1 bay leaf
Salt and freshly ground black pepper
3 tbsps olive or vegetable oil
3 spring onions, finely chopped
90g/3oz mushrooms, sliced
1 tbsp white wine vinegar
Pinch of mixed dried herbs
Cucumber slices, to garnish

Dissolve the agar-agar in the lemon juice. Combine the tomato juice, tomato purée, bay leaf and seasoning in a small saucepan and bring gently to the boil. Allow to stand for 2 minutes, then remove the bay leaf. Stir in the dissolved agar-agar and whisk well to make sure the agar-agar is evenly blended.

Dampen a 700ml/1¼ pint mould or individual moulds and pour in the tomato mixture.

Chill in the refrigerator until set. Heat the oil in a small frying pan and fry the spring onions and mushrooms until soft. Allow the mushrooms to cool completely, then combine them with the vinegar and herbs. Season with salt and pepper. Carefully loosen the tomato chartreuse with a round-bladed knife. Hold a plate over the top of the mould and carefully turn both the plate and the mould over, shaking gently to drop the tomato chartreuse onto the plate. Arrange the mushroom mixture on top and serve garnished with cucumber slices.

Time: Preparation takes about 10 minutes, plus setting. Cooking takes about 5 minutes.

Courgette and Carrot Terrine

This colourful terrine makes a sophisticated starter which is sure to impress family or guests.

SERVES 6-8

6-8 large, green cabbage leaves

1-2 carrots, peeled and cut into thin sticks

1-2 courgettes, cut into thin sticks

340g/12oz low-fat curd cheese

4 slices white bread, crusts removed, made into crumbs

2 eggs, beaten

140ml/¼ pint double cream, lightly whipped

2 tbsps snipped fresh chives

Salt and freshly ground black pepper

280ml/½ pint natural yogurt

140ml/¼ pint mayonnaise

2 tomatoes, skinned, seeded and cut into dice

2 tbsps lemon juice or dry white wine

Pinch of sugar (optional)

Trim the thick spine away from the cabbage leaves by cutting a triangular section out of each. Blanch cabbage leaves in boiling water for 2 minutes, then refresh in cold water. Blanch the carrot sticks for 4 minutes in boiling water, then refresh in cold water. Repeat with the courgette, blanching for only 1 minute.

Combine the cheese, breadcrumbs, eggs, cream, chives and seasoning. Mix well. Drain the blanched vegetables well and pat dry with kitchen paper. Leaving at least 5cm/2 inches of leaf hanging over the edges, carefully line a 900g/2lb loaf tin with the cabbage leaves. Overlap each leaf slightly to ensure that no gap appears when the terrine is turned out. Put one quarter of the cheese mixture into the tin and spread out evenly. Place a layer of carrots over the cheese mixture. Top with a quarter of the cheese mixture. Arrange a layer of courgettes over the cheese and top  with some more of the cheese mixture. Repeat until all the vegetable and cheese mixtures are used. Fold the cabbage over the terrine to enclose the filling completely. Cover with a sheet of non-stick baking parchment, then cover with foil. Place in a roasting tin filled with enough hot water to come halfway up the sides of the terrine. Bake in an oven preheated to 160°C/325°F/Gas Mark 3, for 1½ hours or until the terrine feels firm to the touch.

Cool the terrine completely and chill before turning out. Combine the yogurt, mayonnaise, tomatoes, lemon juice or wine, sugar if using, and a little more seasoning to make a sauce. Cut the terrine into slices and serve with the sauce.

Mushrooms and Tofu in Garlic Butter

A quick and delicious starter.

SERVES 4

225g/8oz button mushrooms
2.5cm/1inch fresh root ginger
225g/8oz smoked tofu
120g/4oz butter
4 small cloves garlic, crushed
2 tbsps chopped parsley

Wipe the mushrooms with a damp cloth. Peel and grate the root ginger. Cut the smoked tofu into small 1.5cm/½-inch squares.

Melt the butter in a frying pan. Add the crushed garlic and ginger and fry gently for two minutes. Add the mushrooms and cook gently for 4-5 minutes until the mushrooms are softened. Finally, add the smoked tofu and heat through. Divide between 4 individually heated dishes, sprinkle with chopped parsley and serve at once.

Time: Preparation takes 10 minutes, cooking takes 12 minutes.
Serving Idea: Serve with French bread or crusty wholemeal rolls.
Variation: Substitute asparagus tips for the button mushrooms.

Pamplemousse

A light and tangy starter which is simple to prepare.

SERVES 6

3 large grapefruit
3 red skinned apples
4 sticks celery
24 grapes (black or green)
60ml/4 tbsps double cream

Halve the grapefruit crossways and cut around the inside of the skin to loosen the flesh. Make deep cuts between the segments close to the membranes and remove the segments making sure you do not pierce the skins. Put the segments into a large bowl with any of the juice.

Cut away any remaining membranes from the shells with a pair of kitchen scissors, put the grapefruit shells into a plastic bag and store in the refrigerator. Remove the cores from the well washed apples and  dice but do not peel. Chop the celery finely.

Halve the grapes and remove the seeds. Add the apples, celery and grapes to the grapefruit and stir in the double cream. Refrigerate until required. Just before serving, stir well and pile the mixture into the grapefruit skins. Serve at once.

Time: Preparation takes 10 minutes.
Serving Idea: To make Vandyke grapefruit, snip small V-shapes from the edges of the empty half shells. Serve garnished with fresh mint leaves.

Stuffed Artichokes

Many people shy away from artichokes, but they are simple to prepare and are absolutely delicious.

SERVES 4

4 globe artichokes
15g/¹⁄₂oz butter or margarine
1 shallot, finely chopped
450g/1lb fresh spinach, stalks removed and washed
60g/2oz breadcrumbs
1 egg, beaten
140ml/1¹⁄₄ pint double cream
Pinch each of ground nutmeg and cayenne pepper
Salt
60g/2oz vegetarian Cheddar cheese, finely grated
60ml/4 tbsps double cream

Cut the tops off each artichoke to about halfway down and trim the stalk end to allow the artichoke to sit upright. Trim away any tough outer leaves and cut out as much of the fluffy 'choke' as possible to form a firm shell. Cook in lightly salted, boiling water for about 10 minutes or until the hearts are tender. Drain and cool. Trim any remaining 'choke' away.

Melt the butter or margarine in a large pan and sauté the shallot until soft. Add the spinach with just the water that remains clinging to the leaves after washing. Cover, and cook until the spinach wilts. Remove from the heat, add the breadcrumbs, egg, cream, nutmeg, cayenne and salt. Pile equal amounts into the centre of the artichokes and place in the top of a steamer. Cover and steam for 10 minutes or until the filling just sets.

In a small bowl, mix together the cheese and the remaining cream, then spoon this on top of each of the filled artichokes and steam for 1 minute. Sprinkle with a little ground nutmeg and serve.

Time: Preparation takes about 20 minutes, cooking time is about 25 minutes.
Variation: Use any other variety of vegetarian hard cheese for the topping.

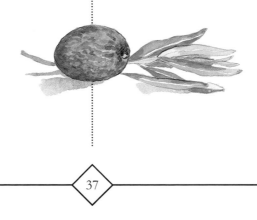

Aubergine Caviar

This novel starter is an interesting and different way of serving this delicious vegetable.

SERVES 4

1 large or 2 small aubergines
Salt
60ml/4 tbsps walnut oil
1 clove garlic, crushed
Juice of 1/2 lemon
Pinch of cayenne pepper
2 hard-boiled eggs (optional)
1 small onion, finely chopped
4-8 slices French bread, toasted
2 tbsps chopped fresh parsley

Remove the stalk from the aubergine and cut in half lengthways. Using a small sharp knife, score and cut the flesh on each half of the aubergine, at about 5mm/1/4-inch intervals, diagonally, first in one direction, then the other. Sprinkle each cut surface with a little salt and leave to stand for 30 minutes, to draw out any bitterness and excess water. Rinse the aubergines thoroughly and pat dry with kitchen paper. Cut the aubergine into chunks. Heat the oil in a frying pan and fry the aubergine and garlic until the aubergine is tender. This will take about 10 minutes.

Place the aubergine in a food processor along with the lemon juice, cayenne and some salt, and process to chop finely. Adjust the seasoning and chill thoroughly.

Cut the eggs in half and separate the yolks from the whites. Push the yolks through a nylon sieve. Finely chop the egg white. Pile the aubergine caviar onto the French bread and top with chopped onion, then egg white, then egg yolk. Sprinkle with chopped parsley and serve.

Time: Preparation takes about 15 minutes, plus standing. Cooking takes about 10 minutes.

Serving Idea: Serve with a side salad.

Variation: Use a 5cm/2-inch piece of cucumber instead of the egg in this recipe, chopping it into very small dice and sprinkling with a little black pepper before using it as a garnish.

Spicy Hot Grapefruit

This simple starter makes an ideal first course, or even a refresher between main courses.

SERVES 4

2 ruby grapefruits
1 tsp ground allspice
2 tsps caster sugar (optional)
Lemon balm or mint leaves, to decorate

Cut the grapefruits in half. Using a small, sharp, serrated knife or a grapefruit knife, cut around the edges of each half between the flesh and the pith. Carefully cut down between each segment and inner thin skins. Take hold of the inner pithy core and gently twist to remove, at the same time pulling away the thin inner skins which have been cut away from the grapefruit segments. Remove any pips. Sprinkle each grapefruit half with equal amounts of the allspice and sugar, if using.

Place under a medium, preheated grill for 3-4 minutes to heat through. Garnish with lemon balm or mint leaves.

Time: Preparation takes about 15 minutes, cooking takes about 5 minutes.

Preparation: The grapefruit halves can be prepared well in advance. Cover closely with cling film to prevent drying out.

Variation: Sprinkle each grapefruit with ground ginger instead of the allspice and pour a teaspoon of ginger wine or sherry over each half.

Cauliflower and Broccoli Soufflettes

Serve as a winter-time starter.

SERVES 6

340g/12oz cauliflower
340g/12oz broccoli
60g/2oz butter or margarine
60g/2oz brown rice flour
420ml/¾ pint milk
60g/2oz vegetarian Cheddar cheese, grated
1 large egg, separated
Good pinch of grated nutmeg

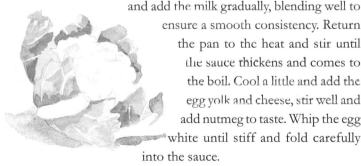

Break the cauliflower and broccoli into small florets and steam until just tender – about 6-8 minutes. Melt the margarine, remove from the heat and gradually add the flour. Stir to a roux and add the milk gradually, blending well to ensure a smooth consistency. Return the pan to the heat and stir until the sauce thickens and comes to the boil. Cool a little and add the egg yolk and cheese, stir well and add nutmeg to taste. Whip the egg white until stiff and fold carefully into the sauce.

Place the vegetables into 6 small buttered ramekin dishes and season. Divide the sauce evenly between the dishes and bake in an oven preheated to 190°C/375°F/Gas Mark 5 for about 35 minutes, until puffed and golden. Serve at once.

Time: Preparation takes 15 minutes, cooking takes 50 minutes.

Mixed Nut Balls

This versatile dish can be made in advance and
refrigerated until required for cooking.

SERVES 8

75g/2¹/₂oz ground almonds
75g/2¹/₂oz ground hazelnuts
75g/2¹/₂oz ground pecan nuts
90g/3oz wholemeal breadcrumbs
120g/4oz vegetarian Cheddar cheese, grated
1 egg, beaten
60-75ml/4-5 tbsps dry sherry or 2 tbsps milk and 3 tbsps dry sherry
1 small onion, finely chopped
1 tbsp grated fresh ginger
1 tbsp chopped fresh parsley
1 small red or green chilli, finely chopped
1 medium red pepper, diced
1 tsp each salt and freshly ground black pepper

Mix the almonds, hazelnuts and pecan nuts together with the
breadcrumbs and the cheese. In another bowl, mix the
beaten egg with the sherry, onion, ginger, parsley, chilli and red
pepper. Combine with the nut mixture and add the salt and
pepper. If the mixture is too dry, add a little more sherry or milk.
Form into small 2.5cm/1-inch balls. Do not preheat the oven.
Arrange the balls on a well greased baking tray and bake at
180°C/350°F/Gas Mark 4 for about 20-25 minutes, until golden
brown.
Time: Preparation takes about 20 minutes, cooking takes 20-25
minutes.

Parsnip Fritters

These tasty fritters make a nice change for lunch
or a light snack.

SERVES 4

120g/4oz plain flour
2 tsps baking powder
1 tsp salt
¹/₂ tsp pepper
1 egg
140ml/¹/₄ pint milk
15g/¹/₂oz melted butter
680g/1¹/₂lbs cooked parsnips, finely diced
Oil or clarified butter for frying

Sift together the flour, baking powder, salt and pepper. Beat the
egg and mix with the milk and melted butter. Stir this mixture
into the dry ingredients. Stir in the cooked parsnips.

Divide the mixture into
16 and shape into small
fritters. Fry in oil or
clarified butter until
browned on both sides.
Time: Preparation takes 10
minutes, cooking takes about 5-8 minutes per batch.
Variation: Courgettes, sweetcorn, onions or aubergine may be
substituted for the parsnips.
Serving Idea: Serve with yogurt sauce or make them slightly larger
and serve as a main course with salad.

Gourmet's Warm Salad

This colourful salad is ideal as a sophisticated starter for a special meal.

SERVES 4

Mixed salad leaves, e.g. frisée, chicory, radicchio,
lamb's lettuce, watercress or iceberg lettuce
2 avocados
175g/6oz black grapes
15g/4 tbsps chopped fresh mixed herbs
120g/4oz walnut pieces
120g/4oz vegetarian blue cheese, diced or crumbled
3 tbsps walnut oil and grapeseed oil, mixed
2 tbsps lemon vinegar
Pinch of sugar

Tear the larger salad leaves into small pieces and place in a large bowl. If using lamb's lettuce, separate the leaves and leave whole. Remove any tough stalks from the watercress. Add all the leaves to the bowl.

Peel the avocados, cut into neat slices and add to the salad leaves. Cut the grapes in half and remove pips; add the grapes to the salad along with the herbs, walnuts and cheese. Put the oils, vinegar and sugar into a screw top jar. Screw down the top well and shake vigorously until the dressing is well blended. Pour the dressing into a large frying pan and heat until bubbling. Quickly add to the salad and toss well, taking care not to break up the avocado.

Arrange on serving plates and serve at once.

Time: Preparation takes about 15 minutes, cooking takes about 2 minutes.

Preparation: It is important to tear the salad leaves by hand as the edges will discolour if they are cut with a knife.

Variation: For a delicious vegan alternative, substitute the cheese with 175g/6oz wild mushrooms that have been cooked in 2 tbsps white wine, drained then chilled.

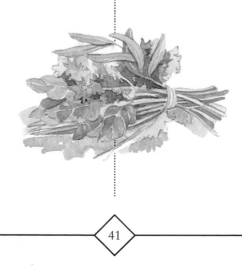

Crudités

A great favourite served with delicious dips to accompany.

SERVES 6-8

Choose from the following vegetable selection:
Cauliflower, broccoli – divided into small florets

Carrots, celery, courgettes, cucumber – cut into matchstick pieces

Chicory – separate the blades

Mushrooms – sliced or quartered

Peppers, kohlrabi, fennel – sliced

Radishes, spring onions, cherry tomatoes – leave whole

Tomato and cheese dip
15g/¹/₂oz butter or margarine

1 tbsp grated onion

225g/8oz tomatoes, skinned and diced

60g/2oz Cheddar cheese, grated

60g/2oz breadcrumbs

1 egg, beaten

¹/₂ tsp mustard powder

Salt and freshly ground black pepper

2-4 tbsps Greek yogurt

Creamed curry dip
1 tbsp mango chutney

90ml/6 tbsps home-made or good quality mayonnaise

1 tsp curry paste

2 tbsps double cream

Pinch of ground cumin

Avocado dip
2 ripe avocados

1 onion, diced

¹/₂ clove garlic, crushed

2 tbsps lemon juice

Salt and freshly ground black pepper

Tomato and Cheese Dip

Melt the butter and gently fry the onion for 2 or 3 minutes until soft. Add the tomatoes, cover and simmer for 10 minutes. Add the cheese, breadcrumbs and egg, and cook for a further minute, stirring all the time, until thickened. Do not allow to boil.

Add the mustard and seasoning and blend or liquidise until smooth. Mix in enough Greek yogurt to ensure a smooth 'dipping' consistency and store in the refrigerator until required.

Creamed Curry Dip

Chop the pieces of mango with a sharp knife and place in a bowl. Add the other ingredients and mix well. Refrigerate until required.

Avocado Dip

Peel the avocados, remove the stones and chop the flesh roughly. Process or liquidise together with the onion, garlic and lemon juice until smooth. Season to taste and refrigerate until required.

Time: Preparation takes 30 minutes, cooking takes 15 minutes.

Stuffed Tomatoes Provençal

A refreshing starter, ideal as a first course to a rich meal.

SERVES 4

4 large ripe tomatoes
30g/1oz butter or margarine
1 clove garlic, crushed
1 shallot, finely chopped
225g/8oz mushrooms, finely chopped
1 tbsp white wine or vegetable stock
45g/1½oz fresh white breadcrumbs
1 tsp chopped fresh parsley
1 tsp chopped fresh basil
¼ tsp dried thyme
1 tsp Dijon mustard
Salt and freshly ground black pepper

Cut the tops off the tomatoes and carefully scoop out the flesh and seeds. Place in a sieve and strain off excess juice. Chop the flesh.

Melt the butter or margarine in a saucepan and sauté the garlic and shallot until soft. Stir in the mushrooms and wine or stock and cook gently for 4 minutes. Remove from the heat and stir in the breadcrumbs, herbs, mustard, seasoning and tomato flesh, mixing well. Fill each tomato with the mixture and place in a shallow ovenproof dish. Place caps on top. Bake in an oven preheated to 180°C/350°F/Gas Mark 4, for 10 to 12 minutes and serve hot.

Time: Preparation takes about 15 minutes, cooking takes about about 15 minutes.

Cee Jay Ratatouille

Cee Jay Ratatouille can be made in advance and reheated before covering with the apples.

SERVES 6

1 medium onion, finely sliced
3 cloves garlic, crushed
60ml/4 tbsps olive oil
1 large aubergine, diced
1 large red pepper, sliced
2 medium courgettes, sliced
4 medium tomatoes, sliced
1 tsp oregano
Salt and freshly ground black pepper
2 large eating apples, thinly sliced
30g/1oz butter or margarine
Ground cloves

Sauté the onion and garlic in the oil until the onion is transparent. Add the aubergine, pepper, courgettes and tomatoes. Cook for a further 5 minutes, stirring occasionally. Add the oregano and seasoning and simmer, covered, for 15-20 minutes.

Divide the ratatouille between 6 heated ovenproof dishes and cover each one with a layer of finely sliced apple. Melt the butter or margarine and brush over the top of the apples. Sprinkle with a good pinch of ground cloves and grill until the apples are brown and fluffy. Serve immediately.

Time: Preparation takes 15 minutes, cooking takes 30 minutes.
Cook's Tip: This dish will happily keep in a moderate oven for up to 30 minutes.

Asparagus with Orange Hollandaise

Simplicity is often the making of a classic dish, and serving fresh asparagus in this way is certainly a classic combination.

SERVES 4

900g/2lbs asparagus spears
Grated rind and juice of ½ orange
Juice of ½ lemon
1 bay leaf
Blade of mace
60g/2oz butter
3 egg yolks, beaten
Salt and freshly ground black pepper
Strips of blanched orange rind, to garnish (optional)

Trim away any thick, tough ends from the asparagus and rinse them well. Bring a sauté pan of lightly salted water to the boil. Move the pan so that it is half on and half off the direct heat (take care not to spill the water). Place the asparagus in the pan so that the tips are in the part of the pan off the direct heat. Cover the pan and bring back to the boil. Cook asparagus for about 10 minutes or until just tender; drain and keep warm.

Meanwhile, prepare the sauce. Heat the orange juice, lemon juice, bay leaf and mace in a small pan to almost boiling and allow to stand for a few moments. Melt the butter in the top of a double boiler or in a bowl placed over a pan of gently simmering water. Whisk the beaten egg yolks into the butter and add the orange rind. Strain the juice into the butter and egg mixture and whisk well. Cook gently until the sauce thickens, whisking constantly.

Once the sauce has reached the desired consistency, immediately remove it from the heat and stand the pan or bowl in cold water to prevent further cooking.

Arrange the asparagus on serving plates and pour equal amounts of sauce over each serving. Garnish with strips of orange rind if wished.

Time: Preparation takes about 10 minutes, cooking takes about 15 minutes.

Serving Idea: Serve with thin slices of wholemeal bread.

Garlic Mushrooms

An established favourite, this can also be served as a light snack.

SERVES 4

60g/2oz butter or olive oil
2 cloves garlic, crushed
¼ tsp chopped fresh thyme
¼ tsp chopped fresh parsley
¼ tsp chopped fresh sage
3 tbsps white wine
Salt and freshly ground black pepper
680g/1½lbs mushrooms, cleaned and quartered
8 slices French bread
2 tbsps snipped chives
Fresh herb sprigs to garnish

Heat the butter or oil in a frying pan and sauté the garlic until soft and beginning to turn golden. Stir in the herbs, wine, seasoning and mushrooms and cook over a low heat for 10 minutes or until the mushrooms are cooked but not too soft.

Warm the bread in a low oven if wished and serve the mushrooms piled onto the bread. Sprinkle with chopped chives and garnish with sprigs of fresh herbs.

Time: Preparation takes about 15 minutes, cooking takes about 15 minutes.

Serving Idea: Serve with sliced tomatoes.

Variation: Wild mushrooms are often available at good greengrocers or in supermarkets; they make a delicious full flavoured variation to this recipe.

Red Lentil Soufflé

Serve this tasty soufflé as a starter or with watercress or salad for a light lunch.

SERVES 4

120g/4oz red lentils
1 bay leaf
280ml/½ pint water
30g/1oz margarine or butter
75ml/2½fl oz double cream
2 egg yolks (size 3)
3 egg whites (size 3)
60g/2oz grated Cheddar cheese (optional)
Salt and pepper
Pinch of paprika

Pick over the lentils and remove any stones. Rinse well. Place the lentils, bay leaf and water in a pan and bring to the boil. Simmer for 20 minutes or until the lentils are soft. Remove the bay leaf and beat the lentils until they are smooth. Beat in the margarine, cream and egg yolks. Beat the egg whites until very stiff and fold into the mixture. Season and fold in the grated cheese. Pour into a well greased soufflé dish and sprinkle with a little paprika. Bake in an oven preheated to 190°C/375°F/Gas Mark 5, for approximately 20 minutes or until the soufflé is well risen, firm and brown. Serve immediately.

Time: Preparation takes about 15 minutes, cooking takes 40 minutes.

Brazilian Avocados

The perfect way to impress your dinner guests right
from the first course.

SERVES 4

2 large, ripe avocados
A little lemon juice
Salt and freshly ground black pepper
60g/2oz finely chopped Brazil nuts
60g/2oz vegetarian Cheddar cheese, grated
2 tbsps vegetarian Parmesan cheese
2 tbsps chopped fresh parsley
2 firm ripe tomatoes, skinned and finely chopped
Wholemeal breadcrumbs
30g/1oz melted butter
A little paprika

Halve the avocados and carefully remove the flesh from the skins. Brush the inside of the skins with a little of the lemon juice. Dice the avocado and put into a bowl with a sprinkling of lemon juice and the seasoning. Add the nuts, cheese, parsley and tomato. Mix gently. Spoon the filling into the avocado shells, sprinkle with the breadcrumbs and drizzle the butter over the top. Dust with the paprika and bake in an oven preheated to 200°C/400°F/Gas Mark 6, for 15 minutes.

Time: Preparation takes about 10 minutes, cooking takes 15 minutes.

Cook's Tip: Do not prepare this dish too far in advance as the avocado may discolour.

Serving Idea: Serve with a little salad as a starter or with baked potatoes, vegetables and tossed salad for a main course.

Celeriac à la Moutarde

This delicious starter could also be served as a light lunch or
supper for two.

SERVES 4

1 large root celeriac, peeled
60g/2oz butter or margarine
30g/1oz plain flour
570ml/1 pint milk
60ml/4 tbsps Dijon mustard
1 tsp celery seasoning
Freshly ground black pepper
30g/4 tbsps dry breadcrumbs

Cut the celeriac into 5mm/¼-inch thick slices and then into sticks about 2.5cm/1-inch long. Cook in lightly salted, boiling water for about 20 minutes or until just tender, then drain.

Meanwhile, melt 45g/1½oz of the butter or margarine in a saucepan. Stir in the flour and cook for about 30 seconds. Remove from the heat and gradually add the milk, stirring well after each addition. Return to the heat and stir in the mustard, celery seasoning and pepper. Cook gently until thickened, stirring constantly. Add the celeriac to the sauce and stir to coat well. Transfer to a serving dish and keep it warm. Melt the remaining butter or margarine in a small frying pan and fry the breadcrumbs until golden. Sprinkle the crumbs over the celeriac and serve immediately.

Time: Preparation takes about 10 minutes, cooking takes about 30 minutes.

Mushroom & Artichoke Salad

Wild mushrooms are becoming more readily available, and this recipe provides a delightful way of serving them.

SERVES 4

2-3 artichokes, depending on size
1 slice of lemon
1 bay leaf
6 black peppercorns
225g/8oz mixed wild mushrooms, e.g. shiitake or oyster
2 tbsps vegetable oil
Radicchio, iceberg lettuce and watercress leaves, mixed
2 tbsps snipped fresh chives
90ml/6 tbsps olive oil
2 tbsps white wine vinegar
1 tbsp Dijon mustard
Salt and freshly ground black pepper
Sprigs fresh dill or chervil, to garnish

Trim the pointed leaves off the artichokes with a sharp knife. Remove the stem. Place the lemon slice, bay leaf and peppercorns in a saucepan of water and bring to the boil. Add the artichokes and cook for 30-40 minutes or until tender and the bottom leaves pull away easily. Stand each artichoke upside-down to drain completely.

Slice the mushrooms. Heat the vegetable oil in a frying pan and fry the mushrooms for 5 minutes, or until just tender. Set aside. Tear the salad leaves into small pieces and place in a bowl with the snipped chives. Whisk together the olive oil, vinegar, mustard and seasoning until thick and pale coloured. Remove the leaves from the drained artichokes and arrange them attractively on plates.

Time: Preparation takes about 20 minutes, cooking time is about 40 minutes.

Preparation: The mushrooms and artichokes can be prepared well in advance and kept in the refrigerator until required.

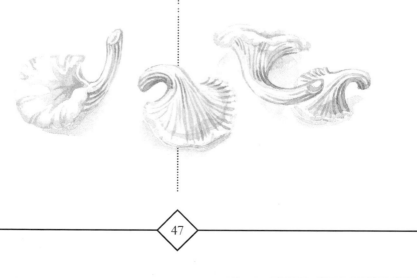

Fennel and Orange Croustade

A delicious mixture which is simple to prepare.

SERVES 4

4 x 2.5cm/1-inch-thick slices wholemeal bread
Oil for deep-frying
2 fennel bulbs (reserve any fronds)
4 oranges
1 tbsp olive oil
Pinch of salt
Chopped fresh mint for garnishing

Trim the crusts off the bread and cut into 7.6cm/3-inch squares. Hollow out the middles, leaving evenly shaped cases. Heat the oil and deep fry the bread until golden brown. Drain the bread well on absorbent kitchen paper. Leave to cool. Trim the fennel bulbs and slice thinly. Place in a mixing bowl. Remove all the peel and pith from the oranges and cut into segments – do this over the mixing bowl to catch the juice.

Mix the orange segments with the fennel. Add the olive oil and salt and mix together thoroughly. Just before serving, divide the fennel and orange mixture evenly between the bread cases and garnish with fresh mint and fennel fronds.

Time: Preparation takes 15 minutes, cooking takes 5 minutes.

Variation: Serve the salad on individual plates sprinkled with croutons.

Cook's Tip: The salad can be made in advance and refrigerated until required but do not fill the cases until just before serving.

Bulgar Boats

This pretty starter can easily be taken on picnics.

SERVES 6

60g/2oz green lentils
120g/4oz bulgar
1 red pepper
1 green pepper
1 medium onion
60g/2oz pine nuts (dry roasted in a pan)
2 tsps dried salad herbs (tarragon, chives or parsley)
Juice and rind of 1 lemon
Salt and freshly ground black pepper
Cos lettuce to serve

Remove any grit or stones from the lentils and rinse well. Cover with plenty of water and boil for about 20 minutes – do not overcook. Place the bulgar wheat in a mixing bowl and cover with boiling water. Leave for about 10 minutes – the grain will then have swollen, softened and absorbed the water.

Dice the peppers and chop the onion finely. Drain the lentils and add to the wheat, together with the peppers, nuts, onion, herbs, lemon juice and rind, salt and pepper. Using one large lettuce leaf per person, spoon the salad into the centre of the leaves and arrange on a large serving dish garnished with wedges of lemon.

Time: Preparation takes 15 minutes, cooking takes 20 minutes.

Variation: Cashews or peanuts could be used instead of pine nuts.

Imam Bayildi

Imam Bayildi means 'the priest has fainted'. Apparently the dish was so delicious that the priest fainted with delight!

SERVES 4

2 large aubergines

Salt

140ml/¹/₂ pint olive oil

2 onions, finely chopped

2 cloves garlic, crushed

250g/9oz tomatoes, skinned and chopped

¹/₂ tsp mixed spice

Juice of ¹/₂ lemon

1 tsp brown sugar

1 tbsp chopped parsley

1 tbsp pine nuts

Salt and freshly ground black pepper

Halve the aubergines lengthways, and scoop out the flesh with a sharp knife, leaving a substantial shell so they do not disintegrate when cooked. Sprinkle the shells with a little salt and leave upside down on a plate for 30 minutes to drain away any bitter juices.

Meanwhile, heat half the oil in a saucepan and fry the onion and garlic until just softened. Add the scooped out aubergine flesh, tomatoes, mixed spice, lemon juice, sugar, parsley, pine nuts and a little seasoning. Simmer for about 20 minutes until the mixture has thickened. Rinse and dry the aubergine shells and spoon the filling into the halves. Place side by side in a buttered ovenproof dish. Mix the remaining oil with 140ml/¹/₄ pint water and a little seasoning. Pour around the aubergines and bake in an oven preheated to 180°C/350°F/Gas Mark 4, for 30-40 minutes or until completely tender.

Time: Preparation takes 25 minutes, cooking takes 1 hour.

Serving Idea: Serve hot or cold garnished with fresh herbs and accompanied by chunks of wholemeal bread. If serving cold, chill for at least 2 hours before serving.

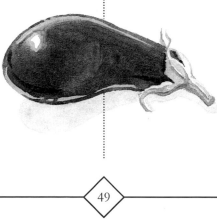

Broccoli and Hazelnut — Terrine —

This colourful, crunchy terrine is full of protein and flavour.

SERVES 6-8

6-8 large whole spinach leaves
450g/1lb broccoli
2 eggs, beaten
175g/6oz low-fat curd cheese
280ml/½ pint double cream, lightly whipped
4 slices white bread, crusts removed, made into crumbs
1 shallot, finely chopped
Pinch of dried thyme
Pinch of ground nutmeg
Salt and freshly ground black pepper
120g/4oz hazelnuts, lightly toasted, then finely chopped
280ml/½ pint mayonnaise
140ml/¼ pint natural yogurt
Grated rind and juice of 1 lemon
Pinch of cayenne pepper

Trim away any coarse stalks from the spinach, taking care to leave the leaves whole. Wash the leaves, blanch in boiling water for 1 minute, drain and refresh in cold water. Drain again and pat dry.

Leaving at least 5cm/2 inches of leaf hanging over the edges, carefully line a 900g/2lb loaf tin with the spinach leaves. Overlap each leaf slightly to ensure that no gaps appear when the terrine is turned out.

Chop the broccoli finely. Put the eggs, cheese, cream, breadcrumbs, shallot, thyme, nutmeg, salt and pepper into a bowl and combine well. Stir in the broccoli and hazelnuts, mixing well to combine thoroughly. Spoon the mixture into the lined loaf tin,  packing it down well, but taking care not to dislodge the spinach leaves. Carefully fold the spinach over the top of the terrine mixture. Cover with a sheet of non-stick baking parchment and then cover with foil. Place in a roasting tin and add enough hot water to come halfway up the sides of the loaf tin. Bake in a preheated oven at 170°C/325°F/Gas Mark 3, for 1 hour, or until the terrine feels firm to the touch.

Cool the terrine completely, and chill before turning out. In a bowl, mix together the mayonnaise, yogurt, lemon rind and juice, cayenne pepper and a little salt. Serve the sauce with slices of the terrine.

Time: Preparation takes abut 20 minutes, cooking takes about 1 hour.

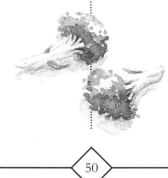

Date, Apple & Celery Starter

A healthy dish with a tasty mix of flavours.

SERVES 4

4 tsps desiccated coconut
2 crisp dessert apples
3-4 sticks celery
90g/3oz dates
2 tbsps natural yogurt
Salt and freshly ground blackpepper
Pinch of nutmeg

Toast the coconut in a dry frying pan over a low heat until it is golden brown, then put to one side. Core and dice the apples and chop the celery finely. Plunge the dates into boiling water, drain and chop finely.

Combine the apples, celery and dates in a mixing bowl. Add the yogurt, seasoning and nutmeg and mix thoroughly so that the salad is coated completely. Transfer to a serving bowl and garnish with the toasted coconut. Serve at once.
Time: Preparation takes 10 minutes, cooking takes 2-3 minutes.
Serving Idea: Serve individual portions on a bed of watercress.
Cook's Tip: Red-skinned apples add colour to this salad.

Hummus

A classic starter which also makes the perfect snack.

SERVES 4

225g/8oz cooked chickpeas (reserve stock)
60ml/4 tbsps light tahini
Juice of 2 lemons
90ml/6 tbsps olive oil
3-4 cloves garlic, crushed
Salt to taste

Put the cooked chickpeas into a blender together with 140ml/¼ pint of the reserved stock. Add the tahini, lemon juice, half of the olive oil, garlic and salt. Blend until smooth, adding a little more stock if it is too thick. Leave to stand for an hour or so to let the flavours develop.

Serve on individual dishes with the remaining olive oil drizzled over the top.
Time: Preparation takes 10 minutes, standing time takes 1 hour.
Serving Idea: Serve sprinkled with paprika and garnished with wedges of lemon.

Salads & Light Meals

Salads are no longer confined to summer's supply of home-grown lettuce, cucumber and tomato. A huge array of fresh ingredients is now available all the year round to make crisp, colourful salads a permanent feature on everyone's menu. Greengrocers and supermarkets are bursting with a wide choice of lettuce and other salad leaves, imported and home-grown, to make the basis of lovely salad bowls – and never has there been a wider choice of tomatoes, from the tiniest cherry to the plump plum variety. Add to these any number of different fresh vegetables, fruit and herbs, raw or lightly cooked, and the scope for salads has never been greater.

With the growing acceptance of the importance of fresh fruit and vegetables in the diet, the inclusion of salad in the daily diet makes sound health sense. For more substantial salads add cooked beans or lentils, grains, nuts, cheese (especially feta or blue cheese) or eggs to turn a side dish into a main course meal.

The choice of dressing can also change the character of a salad. There is a good choice of commercial salad dressings available from shops and these do save time, but for regular salad eaters, it's worthwhile investing in a quality salad oil and one or two speciality vinegars to enable you to experiment with basic dressing recipes. The foundation of a good salad dressing is a good quality oil. Virgin oils are obtained from a plant's first pressing, giving the best flavour, and not surprisingly these are the priciest. Good quality virgin olive oil is a perfect basis for dressings, while speciality oils such as walnut, hazelnut, sesame or almond add their own distinctive flavours. Vinegars too come in many different flavours, from the basic cider and wine vinegars to the exotic, expensive balsamic vinegar or the vibrant flavoured vinegars.

Always remember to dress leafy salads just before serving, but to toss hot ingredients in the dressing as soon as they are cooked to allow flavours to be well absorbed. Salads can make wonderful light meals in themselves as can other dishes based on vegetables, such as the classic ratatouille (p. 60), the humble baked potato, pasta dish or rissotto. There's plenty of scope for meals which bridge the gap between snack and main meal.

Greek Salad

A great favourite which has the added advantage of being easy to prepare.

SERVES 4

2 tomatoes
½ green pepper
¼ cucumber
2 sticks celery, finely sliced
1 tsp fresh basil, finely chopped
Few crisp leaves of lettuce
120g/4oz vegetarian Feta cheese, diced
16 black olives
Dressing
60ml/4 tbsps olive oil
2 tbsps lemon juice
1 clove garlic, crushed
Large pinch of oregano
Salt and freshly ground pepper

Cut each tomato into eight pieces and put into a large mixing bowl. Chop the pepper and cucumber roughly. Add to the tomato together with the celery and chopped basil. Mix together the oil, lemon juice, garlic, oregano and seasoning, and pour over the salad. Mix well to coat all the vegetables.

Arrange a few leaves of lettuce in the bottom of a serving bowl and pile the salad on the top, followed by the cheese cubes. Garnish with olives.

Time: Preparation takes 15 minutes.
Serving Idea: Serve with pitta bread.
Variation: Add a few croutons just before serving.

Fresh & Dried Beans — Provençale —

This attractive dish is full of flavour and is high in protein too.

225g/8oz dried flageolet beans, soaked
450g/1lb tomatoes, skinned and chopped
1 clove garlic, crushed
2 tsps dried basil
1 tsp dried oregano
½ tsp dried rosemary
450g/1lb fresh or frozen green beans, trimmed

Drain the beans and place in a saucepan with enough fresh water to cover them by 2.5cm/1 inch. Bring to the boil, boil rapidly for 10 minutes, then reduce the heat and simmer gently for 1-1½ hours or until the beans are soft. Drain and set aside until required.

Place the tomatoes, garlic and herbs in a saucepan and cook over a low heat for 10 minutes or until the tomatoes soften and the juice begins to flow. Cut the green beans into 2.5cm/1-inch lengths and add to the pan along with the cooked flageolet beans. Cook gently for 15 minutes or until the flavours are well combined.

Time: Preparation takes about 15 minutes, plus about 3 hours soaking. Cooking takes about 2 hours.
Cook's Tip: Canned flageolet beans are now easily available and require no pre-cooking, so reduce the overall cooking time dramatically. Use 450g/1lb canned, drained beans in this recipe.
Serving Idea: Serve this casserole over cornmeal or cooked rice.

Smoked Tofu Salad

Serve this tasty main course salad with granary bread.

SERVES 4-6

225g/8oz broccoli florets
120g/4oz mushrooms
120g/4oz pineapple
60ml/4 tbsps sweetcorn
60-90ml/4-6 tbsps French dressing
1 packet smoked tofu, cut into cubes

Cover the broccoli florets with boiling water and leave to stand for 5 minutes. Drain and allow to cool. Wipe the mushrooms with a clean cloth and slice thinly.

Cut the pineapple into small pieces. Put the broccoli, mushrooms, pineapple and sweetcorn into a large bowl together with the French dressing. Mix carefully. Divide the salad between 4 individual dishes and place the smoked tofu on top. Serve at once.

Time: Preparation takes 15 minutes.

Variation: Omit the tofu and serve as a side salad with savoury flans.

Cook's Tip: If using plain tofu, marinate for a few hours in equal parts of shoyu sauce and olive oil, together with 1 crushed clove of garlic and 1 tsp of fresh grated ginger.

Green Pepper Salad

Serve in individual dishes as a starter accompanied by crusty brown bread or as a light lunch with bread and chunks of cheese.

SERVES 4-6

3 medium green peppers
3 medium tomatoes
2 medium onions
90g/3oz sprouted lentils
Black grapes for garnish
Dressing
60ml/4 tbsps olive oil
2 tbsps red wine vinegar
2 tsps ground cumin
½ tsp fresh coriander, chopped

Core and slice the peppers finely. Slice the tomatoes and onions. Arrange the peppers, tomatoes and onions alternately on a round serving dish and sprinkle the lentil sprouts over the top. Mix all the ingredients for the dressing together well and pour over the vegetables. Cover and leave to marinate for at least 1 hour at room temperature before serving. Just before serving, garnish with halved black grapes.

Time: Preparation takes 10 minutes. Standing takes 1 hour.

Cook's Tip: You can prepare this salad in advance and refrigerate until required but remove from the refrigerator 30 minutes before serving.

Pasta & Asparagus Salad

This elegant green salad is a wonderful way of making the most of asparagus, that most luxurious of vegetables.

SERVES 4

120g/4oz tagliatelle

450g/1lb asparagus, trimmed and cut into 2.5cm/1-inch pieces

2 courgettes, cut into 5cm/2-inch sticks

2 tbsps chopped fresh parsley

2 tbsps chopped fresh marjoram

1 lemon, peeled and segmented

Grated rind and juice of 1 lemon

90ml/6 tbsps olive oil

Pinch of sugar

Salt and freshly ground black pepper

Crisp lettuce leaves

Frisée leaves

Cook the pasta in plenty of lightly salted, boiling water for 10 minutes or as directed on the packet. Drain and refresh in cold water. Drain again and leave to cool completely.

Cook the asparagus in lightly salted, boiling water for 4 minutes, then add the courgettes and cook for a further 3-4 minutes or until the vegetables are just tender. Drain and refresh in cold water. Drain again and leave to cool. Pile the cooked pasta, vegetables, herbs and lemon segments into a large bowl and mix together, taking care not to break up the vegetables.

Mix together the lemon rind and juice, oil, sugar and salt and pepper, to make the dressing. Arrange the lettuce and frisée on serving plates. Just before serving, pour the dressing over the vegetables and pasta and toss to coat well. Pile equal quantities of the pasta salad into the centre of the salad leaves and serve immediately.

Time: Preparation takes about 15 minutes, plus cooling, cooking time is about 20 minutes.

Cook's Tip: Put the ingredients for the dressing into a screw-top jar and shake vigorously to blend thoroughly.

Lollo Rosso Salad

A colourful variation of a Greek Salad.

SERVES 4

¹/₂ Lollo Rosso lettuce
3 medium tomatoes, diced
1 red pepper, chopped
1 green pepper, chopped
3 sticks celery, diced
¹/₃ cucumber, diced
175g/6oz vegetarian Cheshire cheese
16 black olives
Dressing
1 tbsp tarragon vinegar
3 tbsps olive oil

Wash the lettuce and dry it well. Break into pieces with your fingers and put it into a large bowl. Add the tomatoes, pepper, celery, cucumber and cheese. Mix together the vinegar and olive oil, and pour over the salad. Mix gently.

Divide the salad between 4 individual dishes and place 4 olives on the top of each one.

Time: Preparation takes about 10 minutes.
Serving Idea: Serve for lunch with crusty rolls or French bread.
Variation: If you do not like olives, substitute halved, de-seeded black grapes.
Cook's Tip: To keep celery crisp, wash well and place the sticks in a jug of cold water in the refrigerator.

Cucumber Salad

Finely chopped celery may be used in place of fennel in this recipe.

SERVES 6

1 whole cucumber
1 red apple
1 medium fennel bulb, fronds reserved for decoration
1 tbsp pine nuts
Dressing
3 tbsps corn oil or sunflower oil
2 tbsps cider vinegar
2 tbsps fresh dill or 1 tsp dried dill
1 tsp caraway seeds
1-2 tsps paprika
Salt and freshly ground black pepper to taste

Wash the cucumber but do not peel. Cut it very thinly and place the slices in a sieve. Leave to drain for about 20 minutes. Wash and core the apple and slice thinly. Wash and trim the fennel, removing the tough outer leaves and stem. Slice finely.

Combine all the ingredients for the dressing and mix well. Mix with the drained cucumber slices, apple and fennel. Place the salad in the refrigerator or keep in a cool place for about an hour before serving.

Time: Preparation takes 30 minutes.
Serving Idea: Serve decorated with finely chopped fennel leaves and one tablespoon of pine nuts.

Butter Bean, Lemon and Fennel Salad

This interesting combination of textures and flavours makes an unusual lunch or supper dish.

SERVES 4

225g/8oz butter beans, soaked overnight

1 lemon

1 large bulb fennel, thinly sliced

60ml/4 tbsps vegetable or soya oil

Pinch of sugar

Salt and freshly ground black pepper

Lettuce and radicchio leaves, to serve

Place the butter beans in a saucepan, add enough water to cover them by 2.5cm/1 inch and bring to the boil. Boil rapidly for 10 minutes, reduce the heat and simmer gently for about 2 hours or until the beans are tender. Drain well.

Pare the rind from the lemon, taking care not to include too much white pith. Cut the rind into very thin strips. Blanch the lemon rind for 5 minutes in boiling water, then remove with a draining spoon to kitchen paper. Add the fennel to the water (reserve the green tops) and blanch for 2 minutes, the fennel should be just cooked but still crunchy to the bite. Squeeze the juice from the lemon and place in a bowl with the lemon rind strips, oil, sugar and seasoning and whisk together well with a fork. Chop the fennel tops and add to the dressing. Mix the cooked beans and fennel in a large bowl, then add the dressing and toss to coat. Serve on a bed of lettuce and radicchio leaves.

Time: Preparation takes about 10 minutes, plus soaking. Cooking takes about 2 hours.

Black-Eyed Bean and Orange Salad

This colourful salad has a fresh taste which is given a delicious peppery 'bite' by the addition of watercress.

SERVES 4

225g/8oz black-eyed beans, soaked

1 bay leaf

1 slice of onion

Grated rind and juice of 1 orange

75ml/5 tbsps olive or grapeseed oil

6 black olives, pitted and quartered

4 spring onions, trimmed and chopped

2 tbsps each chopped fresh parsley and basil

Salt and freshly ground black pepper

4 whole oranges

1 bunch watercress, washed

Place the beans, bay leaf and onion slice into a saucepan, add enough water to cover by 2.5cm/1 inch and bring to the boil. Boil rapidly for 10 minutes, reduce the heat and simmer gently for about 50 minutes–1 hour, until the beans are tender.

Put the orange rind, juice and oil in a large bowl and whisk together with a fork. Stir in the olives, spring onions and herbs. Add the drained beans to the dressing and season. Mix thoroughly to coat the beans well. Peel and segment the oranges; chop the flesh of 3 of the oranges and add to the beans.

Arrange the watercress on plates and pile equal amounts of the bean and orange salad on top. Arrange the remaining orange segments on the plate and serve immediately.

Time: Preparation takes about 20 minutes, plus soaking. Cooking takes about 1 hour.

Mushroom Croquettes

These tasty croquettes are served with a lightly spiced cream sauce.

SERVES 4

45g/1¹/₂oz butter or vegetable margarine
2 shallots, peeled and finely chopped
120g/4oz mushrooms, finely chopped
45g/1¹/₂oz plain flour
140ml/¹/₄ pint milk
90g/3oz fresh breadcrumbs
1 tsp each chopped fresh parsley and thyme
1 free-range egg, beaten
Salt and freshly ground black pepper
Dry breadcrumbs for coating
Oil for shallow frying
2 tbsps dry vermouth or white wine
280ml/¹/₂ pint double cream
2 tbsps green peppercorns in brine, drained
¹/₂ red pepper, seeded and diced

Melt half the butter or margarine in a frying pan and stir in 1 shallot and the mushrooms. Sauté for 5 minutes or until softened. Stir in 30g/1oz flour and cook for 1 minute. Remove from the heat and gradually beat in the milk. Return to the heat and cook until thickened. Stir in the breadcrumbs, parsley, thyme and half the egg. Season and mix to form a thick paste. Add extra breadcrumbs if it is too thin, and chill well.

Divide into 12 and shape into small ovals with lightly floured hands. Dip in the remaining egg and coat in dry breadcrumbs. Shallow fry for 3 minutes on each side until golden. Meanwhile, heat the remaining fat and shallot in a pan until softened. Stir in the remaining flour, whisk in the vermouth or wine and cream. Season to taste. Cook until thickened slightly. Stir in the peppercorns and red pepper and cook for 1 minute. Serve with a little sauce poured over them.

Time: Preparation takes about 30 minutes, plus chilling.

Cooking takes about 10 minutes.

Vegetarian Suitability: This recipe is suitable for lacto-vegetarians.

Serving Idea: Serve with a watercress and orange salad.

Spinach Salad

Serve with a simple main course.

SERVES 4-6

450g/1lb spinach
1 medium red cabbage
1 medium onion
120g/4oz apricots
90ml/6 tbsps French dressing
60g/2oz toasted sunflower seeds

Wash the spinach and drain well. First remove the outer leaves and core, then slice the cabbage finely. Slice the onion finely and cut the apricots into slivers. Tear the spinach leaves into bite-sized pieces and put into a serving dish. Add the sliced cabbage, onion and apricots. Pour over the dressing and mix together thoroughly. Sprinkle with sunflower seeds and serve.

Time: Preparation takes 15 minutes.

Watchpoint: Spinach leaves bruise easily so take care when washing and tearing the leaves.

Cook's Tip: If using dried apricots, soak beforehand in a little fruit juice.

Ratatouille

This delicious classic dish is equally good served hot or cold.

SERVES 4-6

1 large aubergine
Salt
2 tbsps olive oil
1 large onion, thinly sliced
1 clove garlic, crushed
1 green pepper, thinly sliced
450g/1lb tomatoes, skinned and chopped
1 tsp chopped fresh thyme
2 tsps chopped fresh basil
Salt and freshly ground black pepper
Sprigs of fresh thyme, to garnish

Cut the aubergine in half lengthways and score the cut surface in a diamond fashion with a sharp knife. Sprinkle liberally with salt and allow to stand for 30 minutes, to remove excess moisture. Rinse well and pat dry with kitchen paper. Cut the aubergine halves into thin slices.

Heat the oil in a large frying pan and fry the onion and garlic until it begins to soften, but not brown. Add the pepper and aubergine and sauté for 5 minutes. Stir in the remaining ingredients and cook gently for 30 minutes. Adjust seasoning if required and serve hot or cold. Garnish with a sprig of fresh thyme.

Time: Preparation takes about 20 minutes, plus standing. Cooking takes about 50 minutes.

Stuffed Potatoes

An unusual way of serving this popular vegetable meal.

SERVES 4

4 large baking potatoes, scrubbed
4 eggs
60g/2oz butter or margarine
120g/4oz button mushrooms, sliced
1 shallot, finely chopped
1 tbsp plain flour
420ml/³/₄ pint milk
60g/2oz vegetarian Cheddar cheese, grated
Pinch each of mustard powder and cayenne pepper
Salt and freshly ground black pepper
1 bunch watercress, chopped
Grated cheese, cayenne and watercress, to garnish

Preheat the oven to 200°C/400°F/Gas Mark 6. Prick the potatoes a few times with a fork and place them directly on the oven shelves. Bake for ³/₄-1 hour, or until soft when squeezed. Reduce the oven temperature to 170°C/325°F/Gas Mark 3 and keep potatoes warm.

Poach the eggs in gently simmering water for 3½-5 minutes until the white and yolk is just set. Remove from the pan and keep in cold water. Melt 15g/½oz of the butter or margarine in a small pan and fry the mushrooms and shallot for 5 minutes until just beginning to soften. Melt the remaining fat in another pan, stir in the flour and cook for about 1 minute. Remove from the heat and gradually add 280ml/½ pint of the milk, stirring well after each addition. Return to the heat and cook gently until sauce thickens. Stir in the cheese, and continue cooking until cheese melts. Add the mustard, cayenne, salt and pepper.

When the potatoes are cooked, cut a slice off the top and scoop out the flesh with a spoon, leaving a border to form a firm shell. Put equal amounts of the mushroom mixture into each potato and top with a well drained egg. Spoon the cheese sauce mixture over the top. Heat the remaining milk, until almost boiling. Mash the potato flesh, then gradually beat in the hot milk and watercress. Pipe or spoon the potato over the sauce in the potato shell.

Sprinkle the top with a little extra cheese and return to the oven for 15 minutes to warm through. Serve garnished with cayenne and watercress.

Time: Preparation takes about 20 minutes, cooking takes about 1½ hours.

Serving Idea: Serve with coleslaw or any other salad.

Seeli Salad

Serve this attractive salad for a party or as part of a buffet.

SERVES 4-6

1 large red cabbage
1 green pepper, chopped
½ small pineapple, peeled and finely chopped
Segments from 2 medium oranges
6 spring onions, finely chopped
3 sticks celery, chopped
90g/3oz hazelnuts, roughly chopped
90g/3oz sprouted aduki beans
Dressing
120ml/4fl oz mayonnaise
60ml/2fl oz Greek yogurt
Salt and freshly ground black pepper

Remove any tough or discoloured outer leaves from the cabbage. Remove the base so that the cabbage will stand upright, and cut about a quarter off the top. Using a sharp knife, scoop out the inside of the cabbage leaving 0.6m/¼ inch for the shell. Set the shell aside.

Discard any tough pieces and shred the remaining cabbage very finely. Put the shredded cabbage into a large bowl together with the pepper, pineapple, orange segments, spring onions, celery, hazelnuts and beans. Mix the mayonnaise, yogurt and seasoning together and carefully fold into the vegetables and fruit. Put the mixture into the cabbage shell and place on a serving dish garnished with parsley.
Time: Preparation takes 20 minutes.

Kensington Salad

Decorate the top of this salad with a line of sliced strawberries or kiwi fruit.

SERVES 4-6

3 large mushrooms, thinly sliced
1 dessert apple, cut into chunks and coated with lemon juice
2 celery sticks, cut into matchsticks
30g/1oz walnut pieces
1 bunch watercress
Dressing
1 tbsp mayonnaise
1 tbsp thick natural yogurt
½ tsp herb mustard
A little lemon juice
Salt and freshly ground black pepper

Place the mushrooms, apple, celery and walnuts in a bowl. Combine all the ingredients for the dressing and mix gently with the vegetables. Arrange the watercress on a flat dish or platter and mound the salad mixture on the top.
Time: Preparation takes about 10 minutes.
Variation: A medium bulb of fennel, finely sliced, could be used in place of the celery.

Wheatberry Salad

This substantial salad dish provides an almost perfect protein balance.

SERVES 4

225g/8oz wheatberries, cooked
120g/4oz kidney beans, cooked
3 medium tomatoes
4 spring onions, chopped
2 sticks celery, chopped
1 tbsp pumpkin seeds
Dressing
60ml/4 tbsps olive or sunflower oil
2 tbsps red wine vinegar
1 clove garlic, crushed
1 tsp grated fresh root ginger
1 tsp paprika
1 tbsp shoyu (Japanese soy sauce)
Fresh or dried oregano, to taste
Freshly ground black pepper

Mix the salad ingredients together, reserving a few pumpkin seeds and spring onions for garnishing. Shake the dressing ingredients together in a screw-topped jar. Pour over the salad and mix gently.

Time: Preparation takes 20 minutes.

Serving Idea: Serve with a lettuce salad. Wheatberries also mix well with grated carrot and an orange dressing.

Cook's Tip: This salad keeps well so it can be made in advance and kept in the refrigerator until required.

Tabouleh

This is a traditional salad from the Middle East. The main ingredient is bulgar – partially cooked cracked wheat – which only needs soaking for a short while before it is ready to eat.

SERVES 6

175g-200g/6-7oz bulgar wheat
1 tsp salt
340ml/12fl oz boiling water
450g/1lb tomatoes, chopped
1/2 cucumber, diced
1/2 spring onions
Dressing
60ml/4 tbsps olive oil
60ml/4 tbsps lemon juice
2 tbsps chopped fresh mint
15g/4 tbsps chopped fresh parsley
2 cloves garlic, crushed

Mix the bulgar wheat with the salt, pour over the boiling water and leave for 15-20 minutes. All the water will then be absorbed. Mix together the ingredients for the dressing and pour over the soaked bulgar. Fold in lightly with a spoon. Leave for two hours or overnight in a fridge or cool place. Add the salad ingredients and serve.

Time: Preparation takes about 20 minutes, standing takes about 2 hours.

Cook's Tip: A few cooked beans can be added to make this dish more substantial.

Serving Idea: Serve with flans, cold pies and roasts.

Chickpeas and Bulgar Wheat

High in protein and flavour, this simple lunch dish is sure to become a family favourite.

1 tbsp vegetable oil
2 small onions, peeled and chopped
1 red pepper, seeded and chopped
450g/1lb cooked chickpeas
120g/4oz bulgar wheat
120ml/4fl oz tomato purée
420ml/1¼ pint vegetable stock or water
Onion rings, to garnish

Heat the oil in a saucepan and fry the onions and pepper until soft but not coloured. Stir in the chick peas and bulgur wheat. Stir in the tomato purée, then gradually add the stock or water.

Bring gently to the boil, cover, and simmer gently for 10-15 minutes or until the bulgur wheat is tender and the liquid has been absorbed. Transfer to a serving dish and garnish with onion rings.
Time: Preparation takes about 10 minutes, cooking takes about 20 minutes.
Serving Idea: Serve with a crunchy carrot and peanut coleslaw.
Vegetarian Suitability: This recipe is suitable for vegans.
Cook's Tip: The chickpeas should be boiled for at least 30 minutes. As an alternative, use 450g/1lb canned chickpeas, which will require no pre-cooking.
Variation: Use green peppers in place of the red peppers in this recipe, and add ½ tsp chilli powder for a spicy variation.

Bavarian Potato Salad

It is best to prepare this salad a few hours in advance to allow the potatoes to absorb the flavours.

SERVES 4-6

900g/2lbs tiny new potatoes
60ml/4 tbsps olive oil
4 spring onions, finely chopped
1 clove garlic, crushed
2 tbsps fresh dill, chopped or 1 tbsp dried
2 tbsps wine vinegar
½ tsp sugar
Salt and freshly ground black pepper
2 tbsps chopped fresh parsley

Wash the potatoes but do not peel; put them into a pan, cover with water and boil until just tender. Whilst the potatoes are cooking, heat the olive oil in a frying pan and cook the spring onions and garlic for 2-3 minutes until they have softened a little. Add the dill and cook gently for a further minute. Add the wine vinegar and sugar, and stir until the sugar melts. Remove from the heat and add a little seasoning. Drain the potatoes and pour the dressing over them whilst they are still hot. Allow to cool and sprinkle with the parsley before serving.
Time: Preparation takes 15 minutes, cooking takes 15 minutes.
Serving Idea: Serve with cold roasts.

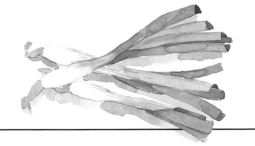

Pasta Primavera

Primavera is Italian for springtime, and this recipe certainly tastes best when tender young spring vegetables and herbs are used.

SERVES 4

450g/1lb pasta shapes
225g/8oz asparagus
120g/4oz green beans, trimmed and cut into diagonal slices
2 carrots, peeled and sliced
60g/2oz butter or margarine
60g/2oz mushrooms, sliced
3 tomatoes, skinned, seeded and chopped
6 spring onions, trimmed and sliced
140ml/¼ pint double cream
Salt and freshly ground black pepper
2 tbsps chopped fresh parsley
2 tsps chopped fresh tarragon

Cook the pasta in plenty of lightly salted, boiling water for 10 minutes or as directed on the packet. Meanwhile, trim any wood ends from the asparagus and cut each spear diagonally into 2.5cm/1-inch pieces, leaving the actual tips whole.

Blanch the asparagus, beans and carrots for 3 minutes in boiling water, then drain well. Melt the butter or margarine in a large pan and add the blanched vegetables and mushrooms. Sauté for 3 minutes, then stir in the tomatoes and spring onions. Add the cream, seasoning and herbs and bring to the boil. Boil rapidly for a few minutes until the cream thickens slightly. When the pasta is cooked, drain well and add to the pan, toss to combine all the ingredients thoroughly and serve immediately.

Time: Preparation takes about 15 minutes, cooking takes 20 minutes.
Variation: Use wild mushrooms in place of the button mushrooms.
Serving Idea: Serve with garlic bread and a tomato salad.

Red Bean Creole

This bright and colourful dish is ideal served on its own
or as part of a larger meal.

SERVES 4

175g/6oz long-grain brown or white rice
30g/1oz butter or vegetable margarine
1 green pepper, seeded and sliced
120g/4oz mushrooms, sliced
Pinch of cayenne pepper
Pinch of ground nutmeg
340g/12oz cooked red kidney beans
140ml/¼ pint vegetable stock
4 firm tomatoes, skinned, seeded and cut into strips
4 spring onions, trimmed and chopped
Salt and freshly ground black pepper
Chopped fresh parsley, to garnish

Cook the rice in plenty of lightly salted, boiling water as
directed on the packet. Drain the rice and rinse under boiling
water. Melt the butter or margarine in a large saucepan and sautée
the pepper and mushrooms for 5 minutes or until just
beginning to soften. Add the rice, cayenne, nutmeg,
beans and stock. Cook gently for 10 minutes, stir in
the remaining ingredients and cook for a further
5 minutes or until all the ingredients are heated
through.

Serve garnished with chopped parsley. This dish is
delicious served with Ratatouille.
Time: Preparation takes about 20 minutes, cooking takes about
40 minutes.

Sunset Salad

Serve this colourful salad with cold nut roasts, raised
pies or quiche.

SERVES 4-6

3 dessert apples
340g/12oz celery
4 medium mushrooms
90g/3oz walnuts
Lettuce leaves
90g/3oz alfalfa sprouts
90g/3oz black grapes
Dressing
120ml/4fl oz mayonnaise
60ml/2fl oz natural yogurt
Salt and freshly ground black pepper

Cut the unpeeled apples into quarters and remove the core.
Dice roughly. Dice the celery and slice the mushrooms.
Chop the walnuts into quarters. Mix the mayonnaise and yogurt
together and season. Put the apples, celery, mushrooms and
walnuts into a bowl and fold in the dressing.

Line a serving dish with well washed lettuce and
spread the sprouts around the outer edge. Pile the
salad in the centre and garnish with the grapes.

Time: Preparation takes 15 minutes.

Cook's Tip: Use red-skinned apples and lettuce
tinged with red (e.g. Lollo Rosso) to give colour to
your salad.

Cucumber & Pineapple Salad

If you do not have fresh pineapple, use tinned pineapple without added sugar.

SERVES 4

4 tsps raisins
2 tbsps pineapple juice
275g/10 oz cucumber
1 red pepper
175g/6oz pineapple
3 tbsps French dressing
1 tsp fresh mint, finely chopped
2 tsps sesame seeds

Soak the raisins in the pineapple juice for at least half an hour. Slice the cucumber finely. Chop the pepper finely. Chop the pineapple into cubes. Arrange the cucumber on a serving dish. Mix the pepper, pineapple and raisins together and pile in the centre of the cucumber.

Mix the mint into the French dressing and pour over the salad just before serving. Sprinkle the sesame seeds over the top. Time: Preparation takes 10 minutes, soaking takes 30 minutes. Serving Idea: Serve with flans and nut roasts.

Macaroni & Blue Cheese

The classic combination of apples and blue cheese sets this delicious variation of macaroni cheese apart from its humble origins.

SERVES 4

340g/12oz wholemeal macaroni
90g/3oz butter or margarine
90g/3oz plain flour
570ml/1 pint milk
1 tsp dried or fresh chopped tarragon
225g/8oz vegetarian blue cheese, crumbled or grated
Salt and freshly ground black pepper
2 tbsps vegetable oil
2 apples, cored and chopped
2 onions, chopped
1 clove garlic, crushed
Sprig of fresh tarragon, to garnish

Cook the macaroni in plenty of lightly salted, boiling water for about 12 minutes. Drain well. Meanwhile, melt the butter or margarine in a saucepan, stir in the flour and cook for 1 minute. Remove from the heat and gradually stir in the milk. Return to the heat and cook gently until the sauce thickens, stirring constantly. Stir in the tarragon and blue cheese and cook until the cheese melts; taste and season with salt if needed and freshly ground pepper. Heat the oil and fry the apples, onions and garlic for 5 minutes until just soft. Mix the apple and onion into the sauce then stir in the drained pasta; return to the heat to warm through the pasta if necessary. Serve garnished with a sprig of fresh tarragon. Time: Preparation takes 5 minutes, cooking takes about 20 minutes.

Red Lentil & Mushroom Loaf

This delicious and highly nutritious vegetable loaf is equally good served hot or cold.

SERVES 4-6

175g/6oz red lentils
340ml/12fl oz vegetable stock or water
1 egg
2 tbsps double cream
90g/3oz mushrooms, chopped
120g/4oz curd or cream cheese
1 clove garlic, crushed
1 tbsp chopped fresh parsley
Salt and freshly ground black pepper
400g/14oz can chopped tomatoes
1 tbsp tomato purée
Pinch of sugar
1 tbsp chopped fresh tarragon

Rinse the lentils and place in a saucepan with the stock or water. Bring gently to the boil, and boil rapidly for 10 minutes. Reduce the heat and continue to cook until the lentils are soft and the liquid has been absorbed.

Using a potato masher, mash the lentils to a thick purée. Beat the egg and cream together and add to the lentil purée, along with the mushrooms, cheese, garlic, parsley and seasoning. Mix all the ingredients together thoroughly. Press the lentil mixture into a greased and lined 450g/1lb loaf tin. Bake in a preheated oven at 180°C/350°F/Gas Mark 4, for 1 hour or until firm to the touch.

Put the tomatoes, tomato purée, sugar and half the tarragon into a small saucepan and cook for 5 minutes. Purée in a food processor or push through a sieve to form a smooth sauce.

Stir in the remaining tarragon and season to taste. Slice the loaf and serve with the tomato sauce and a mixed salad.

Time: Preparation takes about 15 minutes, cooking time is about 1 hour, 20 minutes.

Spaghetti with Pine Nuts

This crunchy, flavoursome combination makes good use of store-cupboard ingredients.

SERVES 4

340g/12oz spaghetti
90ml/6 tbsps olive oil
1 large onion, sliced
1 clove garlic, crushed
120g/4oz pine nuts
400g/14oz can artichoke hearts, drained
2 tbsps chopped fresh parsley
60g/2oz vegetarian Cheddar cheese, grated (optional)

Cook the spaghetti in plenty of lightly salted, boiling water for 10 minutes or as directed on the packet. Just before the spaghetti is cooked, heat the oil in a frying pan and fry the onion and garlic until beginning to brown. Add the pine nuts and cook for 1 minute. Chop the artichoke hearts into bite-sized pieces and add to the pan with the parsley. Heat gently for a few minutes.

When the spaghetti is cooked, drain well and add to the pan. Toss until the spaghetti is well coated in the oil. Stir in the grated cheese if using, reserving a little to sprinkle on top. Transfer to a serving dish and sprinkle with the remaining cheese. Serve immediately.

Time: Preparation takes about 5 minutes, cooking takes about 15 minutes.

Cook's Tip: If fresh pasta is used, start cooking the onion and garlic immediately as the cooking time is much shorter.

Danish Egg Salad

This delicious salad is ideal for a light lunch or supper for two.

SERVES 4

1 egg

1 tbsp single cream

Salt and freshly ground black pepper

Knob of butter or margarine

225g/8oz fresh or frozen peas

280ml/½ pint soured cream

60ml/4 tbsps mayonnaise

2 tbsps chopped fresh dill

Pinch of paprika

Salt

6 sticks celery, trimmed and diced

120g/4oz vegetarian cheese of your choice, diced

120g/4oz diced cucumber

3 spring onions, chopped

½ head Chinese leaves, shredded

Beat together the egg, cream and seasoning in a small bowl. Melt the butter or margarine in a frying pan and pour in the egg mixture; tilt the pan so that the egg coats the base in a thin layer. Cook gently for 1-2 minutes or until the egg is set. Carefully flip over and cook the other side. Remove from the pan and allow to cool.

Cook the peas and refresh in cold water, then drain and set aside. Whisk together the soured cream, mayonnaise, dill, paprika and a little salt. Reserve a few tablespoons. Mix the remaining dressing with the peas, celery, cheese, cucumber and spring onions.

Arrange the Chinese leaves on a serving dish and pile the vegetable mixture into the centre. Using a sharp knife, shred the omelette and use to garnish the salad. Drizzle over the reserved soured cream dressing before serving.

Time: Preparation takes about 20 minutes, cooking takes about 10 minutes.

Variation: Use finely chopped tarragon in place of dill in this recipe and a mild vegetarian brie for a delicious French version.

Pasta and Avocado Salad

The perfect lunch or supper salad for guests.

SERVES 4

225g/8oz pasta shapes

3 tbsps mayonnaise

2 tsps tahini

1 orange

½ medium red pepper, chopped

1 medium avocado

Pumpkin seeds to garnish

Cook the pasta until soft and leave to cool. Mix together the mayonnaise and tahini. Segment the orange and chop into small pieces, retaining any juice. Chop the pepper. Stir the mayonnaise mixture, pepper and orange (plus juice) into the pasta. Just before serving, cube the avocado and stir in carefully.

Serve decorated with pumpkin seeds.

Time: Preparation takes about 10 minutes, cooking takes about 35 minutes.

Watchpoint: Do not peel the avocado until required as it may discolour.

Variation: Green pepper may be used in place of the red pepper.

Vegetable Pilau

Lightly spiced and fragrant, this traditional Indian rice dish will serve 4 as a lunch or supper on its own, or 6 as part of a larger Indian meal.

SERVES 4-6

60g/2oz butter or 60ml/4 tbsps vegetable oil

1 onion, finely sliced

225g/8oz long-grain rice

1 small piece cinnamon stick

4 cardamoms, husks removed and seeds crushed

4 cloves

½ tsp ground coriander

¼ tsp ground turmeric

¼ tsp garam masala

1 bay leaf

Salt and freshly ground black pepper

570ml/1 pint vegetable stock or water

½ aubergine, diced

60g/2oz frozen cauliflower florets

120g/4oz frozen mixed vegetables

Melt the butter or heat the oil in a large saucepan and fry the onion until beginning to soften. Stir in the rice, spices, bay leaf and seasoning and fry for 2 minutes, stirring constantly. Add the stock or water, stir well, bring gently to the boil and cook for 5 minutes. Add the remaining ingredients and cook for a further 5-7 minutes or until rice is tender and most of the liquid has been absorbed. Leave covered for 5 minutes until the remaining liquid has been absorbed. Stir to separate the grains and serve.

Time: Preparation takes 10 minutes, cooking takes about 20 minutes.

Pancakes Provençale

These moreish pancakes are quick and easy to make.

SERVES 4

60g/2oz plain flour
Pinch salt
1 free-range egg
140ml/¼ pint milk
Oil for frying
2 green peppers, seeded and diced
1 red pepper, seeded and diced
1 large onion, peeled and finely chopped
1 clove garlic, crushed
1 small courgette, diced
3 tomatoes, skinned, seeded and chopped
1 tsp chopped fresh basil
2 tbsps tomato purée
30g/1oz vegetarian Cheshire or Wensleydale cheese, crumbled
Salt and freshly ground black pepper
Fresh herbs and tomato slices, to garnish

Put the flour and salt into a bowl. Make a well in the centre and add the egg and a little of the milk. Using a wooden spoon, gradually incorporate the flour into the egg mixture to form a smooth paste. Gradually beat in the remaining milk.

Heat a little oil in a heavy-based frying pan and spoon in a little of the batter; swirl to coat the base of the pan. Cook for about 1 minute or until the underside is golden. Flip or toss the pancake over and cook the other side. Slide the pancake out of the pan and keep warm. Repeat with the remaining batter. You should end up with 8 pancakes. Heat 2 tbsps oil in a small pan and fry the peppers, onion and garlic until beginning to soften. Stir in the courgette and tomatoes and cook for 2 minutes. Add the basil, tomato purée, cheese and seasoning, and cook gently until cheese begins to melt.

Divide the vegetable mixture between the pancakes and roll or fold the pancakes to enclose the filling. Serve immediately garnished with sprigs of fresh herbs and tomato slices.

Time: Preparation takes about 20 minutes, cooking takes about 30 minutes.

Vegetarian Suitability: This recipe is suitable for lacto-vegetarians only. See variation for vegan alternative.

Variation: Omit the cheese from the filling and substitute halved pitta bread for the pancakes to make a vegan variation.

Spinach and Pepper
— Casserole —

This hearty, warm casserole makes a substantial lunch or supper dish, or could be used as an accompanying vegetable for up to 8 people.

450g/1lb spinach, washed, trimmed and roughly chopped
2 tbsps oil
1 red pepper, seeded and sliced
1 green pepper, seeded and sliced
4 sticks celery, trimmed and thinly sliced
2 onions, peeled and finely chopped
30g/1oz sultanas
Pinch paprika
Pinch unrefined sugar
Pinch of ground cinnamon
Salt
2 tbsps tomato purée
1 tsp cornflour
30g/1oz vegetarian Cheddar cheese
2 tbsps fresh breadcrumbs

Cook the spinach in a covered pan until just wilted, with just the water that clings to the leaves after washing. Drain the spinach well, reserving the cooking liquid to make the sauce. Heat the oil in a frying pan and fry the peppers, celery and onions for about 10 minutes, or until softened.

Mix together the sultanas, paprika, sugar, cinnamon, salt, tomato purée and cornflour. Make the reserved cooking liquid up to 140ml/¼ pint and stir into the cornflour mixture. Add to the vegetables and cook, stirring until the sauce thickens. Spoon the vegetable mixture into a flameproof casserole dish. Mix together the cheese and breadcrumbs and sprinkle over the vegetables. Place under a preheated grill until the cheese melts and the crumbs are golden.

Time: Preparation takes about 15 minutes, cooking time is about 20 minutes.

Vegetarian Suitability: This recipe is suitable for lacto-vegetarians only.

Serving Idea: Serve with a rice salad.

Main Meals

Finding something to take the place of meat, fish and fowl for the main meal of the day is probably the biggest challenge facing those new to vegetarian eating. Vegetarian main meals, however, can be just as varied – and delicious – as those eaten conventionally. You can choose from a huge range of different plant foods – nuts, grains, beans, lentils and seeds and all manner of fruit and vegetables, as well as dairy foods such as eggs, milk, yogurt and cheese, where appropriate. There's no lack of raw materials and no shortage of tasty ways of preparing them either.

While vegetarian main course dishes beyond omelettes and cauliflower cheese may be quite new to us, in different countries meat-free dishes have featured prominently for generations. Drawing on the traditions of India and Oriental countries where vegetarianism is an integral feature of the cuisine inspires many delicious dishes, such as Curried Lentils (p. 79), Indian Vegetable Curry (p. 104), Sesame Stir Fry (p. 113) and Green Lentils with Ginger and Spices (p. 97).

Making more use of beans and lentils, grains, nuts and seeds, all relatively rich in protein, is an important part of a balanced vegetarian diet. Simply replacing meat, fish and fowl with more eggs and cheese results in a fat-rich diet. Dairy products are helpful, however, in boosting the protein intake of vegetarians.

One of the keys in balancing a meat-free diet is to try to ensure different protein foods are eaten together at a meal. That means mixing grains, nuts, seeds, beans and lentils with each other or with dairy foods to make for a good balance of protein. Often this happens within a recipe – Nut and Herb Bulgar (p 82), mixes nuts with bulgar, a wheat product, while Beany Lasagne (p.109) combines beans with pasta, another wheat-based product. Pasta lends itself perfectly to vegetarian cooking – there's plenty of scope for serving pasta with traditional tomato-based sauces or dairy sauces as well as experimenting with more contemporary recipes such as Pasta Spirals with Walnuts and Stilton (p. 90). Pastry dishes – quiches, pies and pasties – are also ideal for serving with a vegetarian filling and are often useful standbys to offer to those not familiar with vegetarian eating.

There are occasions when a straight substitute for roast meat or poultry is required and that's when the notorious nut roast comes into its own. The butt of many undeserving jokes, nut roasts should be given a fair chance to prove their delicious flavour. Blended from ground nuts, breadcrumbs and liberal use of herbs, seasonings and often finely chopped vegetables, recipes such as Carrot and Cashew Nut Roast (p.115) or Festive Roast (p. 115) could surprise and impress even die-hard meateaters.

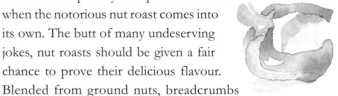

Quick Vegetable Chilli

Serve this tasty chilli with wholemeal baps and salad.

SERVES 4

2 large onions, sliced
1 tbsp olive oil
3-4 cloves garlic, crushed
1 tsp chilli powder
400g/14oz can tomatoes, chopped
400g/14oz can red kidney beans
1 small red pepper, roughly chopped
1 medium courgette, sliced into chunks
Cauliflower florets
2 carrots, roughly chopped
½ tbsp tomato purée
1 tsp dried, sweet basil
1 tsp oregano
¼-½ pint stock

Sauté the onions in the oil until soft. Add the garlic and cook for 1 minute. Add the chilli powder and cook for a further minute. Add the rest of the ingredients and simmer for 25-30 minutes. Serve on a bed of brown rice.
Time: Preparation takes about 15 minutes, cooking takes 30 minutes. Variation: Broccoli florets could be used in place of the cauliflower.

Savoury Rice Cake

An excellent way to use up leftover rice.

SERVES 2-4

1 medium onion, finely chopped
1 clove garlic, crushed
2 tbsps olive oil
1 tbsp fresh thyme, chopped
1 red pepper, thinly sliced
1 green pepper, thinly sliced
4 eggs, beaten
Salt and freshly ground black pepper
6 tbsps cooked brown rice
3 tbsps natural yogurt
90g/3oz vegetarian Cheddar cheese, grated

Fry the onion and garlic in the olive oil until soft. Add the thyme and pepper and fry gently for 4-5 minutes. Beat the eggs with the salt and pepper. Add the cooked rice to the thyme and pepper, followed by the eggs. Cook over a moderate heat, stirring from time to time until the eggs are cooked underneath.

Spoon the yogurt on top of the part-set egg and sprinkle the cheese over the top. Put under a moderate grill and cook until puffed and golden. Serve immediately.
Time: Preparation takes about 15 minutes, cooking takes 15 minutes.
Serving Idea: Garnish with fresh thyme and serve with a green salad.

Courgette & Pine Nut
— Lasagne —

This unusual lasagne will leave your guests curious as to the delicious combination of ingredients.

SERVES 4

12 strips of wholewheat lasagne
90g/3oz pine nuts
30g/1oz butter
675g/1½lbs courgettes, trimmed and sliced
275g/10oz ricotta cheese
½ tsp grated nutmeg
1 tbsp olive oil
1 large aubergine, sliced
140ml/¼ pint water
2 tsps shoyu sauce (Japanese soy sauce)
90g/3oz Cheddar cheese, grated

Place the lasagne in a large roasting tin and completely cover with boiling water. Leave for 10 minutes and then drain. Place the pine nuts in a dry pan and roast gently for 2 minutes. Set aside. Melt the butter and cook the courgettes with a little water until just tender. Combine the courgettes, pine nuts and ricotta cheese. Add the nutmeg and mix together thoroughly.

In a separate pan, heat the olive oil and sauté the aubergine for 4 minutes. Add the water and shoyu and simmer, covered, until soft. Liquidise, adding a little extra water if necessary. Place 4 strips of lasagne on the bottom of a greased 3 pint rectangular dish and top with half the courgette mixture. Place 4 more strips of lasagne over the courgettes and add half the aubergine sauce followed by the rest of  the courgettes. Cover with the remaining lasagne and the rest of the sauce. Sprinkle the grated cheese over the top and bake in an oven preheated to 190°C/375°F/Gas Mark 5, for 40 minutes or until the cheese is golden brown.

Time: Preparation takes about 30 minutes, cooking takes 50 minutes.

Serving Idea: Serve with a crunchy mixed salad and Creamy Jacket Potatoes – bake the potatoes until soft, remove the potato from the skins and mash with a little milk, butter and seasoning. Cool a little and place the mixture in a piping bag with a large nozzle. Pipe the mixture back into the potato shells and re-heat when required.

Note: You will need to cook a couple of extra potatoes in order to have plenty of filling when they are mashed.

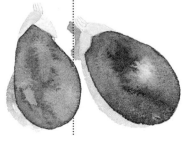

Vegetable Niramish

This highly fragrant curry is ideal to serve as part of a larger Indian meal. Vary the vegetables according to what you have to hand.

SERVES 4

1 small aubergine

Salt

3 tbsps vegetable oil

1 onion, sliced

1 green chilli, seeded and finely chopped

1 tsp cumin seeds

1 large potato, peeled and cut into chunks

120g/4oz cauliflower florets

1 small green pepper, sliced

2 small carrots, peeled and thickly sliced

1 tsp each ground coriander, turmeric and chilli powder

140ml/¼ pint vegetable stock

1 tsp chopped fresh coriander

Juice of 1 lime

Chillies to garnish

Cut the aubergine into chunks, sprinkle liberally with salt, and allow to stand for 30 minutes. Rinse well and drain on kitchen paper.

Heat the oil in a saucepan and fry the onion, green chilli and cumin seeds for 2 minutes. Stir in the potato and fry for 3 minutes. Add the aubergine, cauliflower, pepper and carrots and fry for another 3 minutes. Stir in the spices and fry for 1 minute, then add the stock. Cover and simmer gently for 30 minutes until all the vegetables are tender, adding a little more stock if needed.

Add the coriander and lime juice and simmer for 2 minutes. Serve garnished with chillies.

Time: Preparation takes about 20 minutes, plus standing. Cooking takes about 40 minutes.

Serving Idea: Serve with boiled rice and a simple salad.

Curried Lentils

This curry does take a while to prepare, but is worth the effort.

SERVES 4

225g/8oz brown lentils
60ml/4 tbsps vegetable oil
1 large onion, finely chopped
1 clove garlic, crushed
1 red or green chilli, seeded and finely chopped
1 tsp each ground cumin, coriander and turmeric
½ tsp each ground cinnamon and nutmeg
570ml/1 pint vegetable stock
60g/2oz blanched almonds
Salt and freshly ground black pepper
30g/1oz margarine or oil
2 slightly under-ripe bananas, peeled and sliced
1 tbsp dark brown sugar
2 tbsps lemon juice
Pinch each of nutmeg, cinnamon and garam masala
2 dessert apples, cored and chopped
60g/2oz raisins
120g/4oz cucumber, finely chopped
60ml/4 tbsps mango chutney
2 large tomatoes, skinned and chopped
½ green pepper, finely chopped
4 spring onions, trimmed and sliced
2 tsps walnut oil
Pinch of cayenne pepper
Fresh coriander leaves and desiccated coconut, to garnish

Rinse the lentils under running water and set aside. Heat the oil in a saucepan and fry the onion, garlic and chilli for 3-4 minutes, or until beginning to soften. Stir in the spices and fry for 1 minute. Add the lentils and stock and bring to the boil; cover and cook for 45 minutes or until lentils are soft and most of the liquid has been absorbed. If the lentils are soft but there is a lot of liquid remaining, simmer uncovered for a further 10 minutes to evaporate the liquid. Stir in the almonds. Season to taste. Cover and keep warm.

To make the accompaniments, melt the margarine or oil and cook the banana for 1 minute. Sprinkle with sugar, half the lemon juice, the nutmeg, cinnamon and garam masala. Stir well and transfer to a serving dish. Mix the apple with the raisins, cucumber and chutney and transfer to a serving dish. Mix together the tomatoes, green pepper, spring onions, remaining lemon juice, walnut oil and cayenne. Season and transfer to a serving dish. Serve the curry garnished with coriander leaves, coconut and the accompaniments.

Time: Preparation takes about 50 minutes, cooking takes about 40 minutes.

Vegetable Stir-Fry With Tofu

The inclusion of tofu in the recipe makes it an excellent protein meal.

SERVES 4

4 heads of broccoli
120g/4oz baby corn
60ml/4 tbsps vegetable oil
30g/1oz blanched almonds
1 clove garlic, crushed
1 red pepper, sliced
120g/4oz mange tout peas, trimmed
60g/2oz water chestnuts, sliced
60ml/4 tbsps soy sauce
1 tsp sesame oil
1 tsp sherry
140ml/¼ pint vegetable stock
2 tsps cornflour
120g/4oz bean sprouts
4 spring onions, cut into thin diagonal slices
225g/8oz tofu, cut into cubes
Salt and freshly ground black pepper

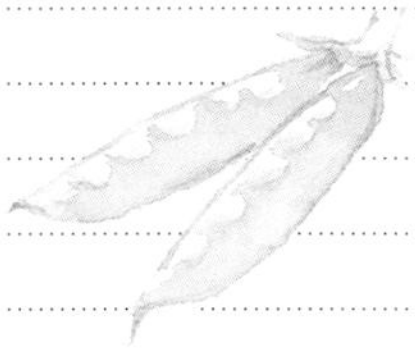

Remove the florets from the broccoli and set aside. Trim the broccoli stems and slice thinly. Cut the baby corn in half lengthways. Heat the oil in a wok or large frying pan and fry the almonds until browned. Remove with a draining spoon and set aside. Add the garlic, broccoli stems and baby corn to the pan and stir-fry for 1 minute. Stir in the pepper, mange tout peas, water chestnuts and broccoli florets and stir-fry for 4 minutes.

Mix the soy sauce, sesame oil, sherry, stock and cornflour together in a small dish and stir until blended. Add to the pan and stir until sauce thickens. Add the bean sprouts, browned almonds, spring onions and tofu and cook for 3 minutes. Season to taste and serve at once.

Time: Preparation takes about 20 minutes, cooking takes about 10-12 minutes.

Serving Idea: Serve with boiled rice or mixed grains and seeds.

Variation: Use any combination of vegetables in season.

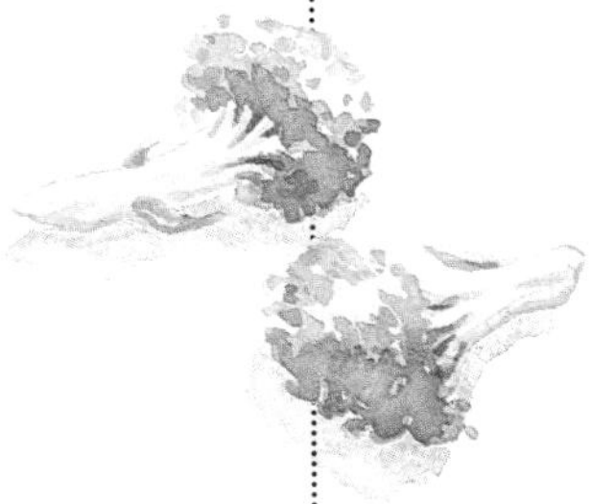

Vegetarian Shepherds Pie

The Shepherds Pie will serve 2 people without any accompaniment and 4 people if served with vegetables.

SERVES 2-4

120g/4oz brown lentils
60g/2oz pot barley
420ml/¾ pint stock or water
1 tsp yeast extract
1 large carrot, diced
½ onion, finely chopped
1 clove garlic, crushed
60g/2oz walnuts, roughly chopped
1 tsp vegetarian gravy powder or thickener
Salt and freshly ground black pepper
450g/1lb potatoes, cooked and mashed

Simmer the lentils and barley in 280ml/½ pint of the stock and yeast extract for 30 minutes. Meanwhile, cook the carrot, onion, garlic and walnuts in the remaining stock for 15 minutes or until tender. Mix the gravy powder or thickener with a little water, add to the carrot mixture and stir over a low heat until thickened.

Combine the lentils and barley with the carrot mixture; season and place in an ovenproof dish. Cover with the mashed potato and bake in an oven preheated to 180°C/350°F/Gas Mark 4, for about 30 minutes until browned on top.
Time: Preparation takes 15 minutes, cooking takes 1 hour.
Serving Idea: Garnish with grilled tomatoes and serve with vegetables in season; broccoli, sprouts, spring cabbage etc.

Oven Baked Spaghetti

A convenient way to cook this favourite mid-week meal.

SERVES 4

225g/8oz wholewheat spaghetti, cooked
2 x 400g/14oz cans tomatoes, roughly chopped
1 large onion, grated
1 tsp oregano
Salt and freshly ground black pepper
120g/4oz vegetarian Cheddar cheese
2 tbsps vegetarian Parmesan cheese, grated

Grease four individual ovenproof dishes and place a quarter of the spaghetti in each one. Pour the tomatoes over the top. Add the onion, sprinkle with oregano and season well. Slice the cheese finely and arrange over the top of the spaghetti mixture.

Sprinkle with Parmesan and bake in an oven preheated to 180°C/350°F/Gas Mark 4, for 30 minutes.
Time: Preparation takes 10 minutes, cooking takes 20-25 minutes.
Serving Idea: Serve with garlic bread.
Watchpoint: When cooking spaghetti remember to add a few drops of oil to the boiling water to stop it sticking together.
Cook's Tip: Oven Baked Spaghetti may be cooked in one large casserole if required but add 10 minutes to the cooking time.

Tri-Coloured Tagliatelle & Vegetables

A delicious Italian dish that is ideal for an informal supper party.

SERVES 4

225g/8oz tri-coloured tagliatelle (mixture of tomato,
spinach and egg pasta)
60g/2oz butter or margarine
1 large onion, sliced
225g/8oz broccoli florets
2 red peppers, sliced
2 cloves garlic, crushed
2 tsps chopped fresh rosemary
90g/3oz vegetarian Cheddar cheese, finely grated
Salt and freshly ground black pepper

Cook the pasta in plenty of lightly salted, boiling water for 10 minutes or as directed on the packet. Meanwhile, melt half the butter or margarine in a frying pan, add the onion and sauté for 4 minutes. Add the broccoli and peppers and continue to cook for 5 minutes or until all the vegetables are tender.

Place the garlic, rosemary and remaining fat in a separate saucepan and heat gently for a few minutes until the fat melts and the flavours combine. When the pasta is cooked, drain well and return to the pan. Strain the garlic mixture through a sieve onto the pasta – this gives a very subtle hint of garlic and rosemary to the pasta. Add the cooked vegetables and cheese. Season to taste and toss well before serving.

Time: Preparation takes about 10 minutes, cooking takes about 15 minutes.

Nut & Herb Bulgar

Bulgar wheat cooks in a similar way to rice and can be used as an alternative to many rice dishes.

SERVES 4

1 tbsp walnut oil
1 tbsp vegetable oil
1 red pepper, cut into short sticks
1 onion, chopped
30g/1oz pine nuts
120g/4oz cucumber, diced
1 tbsp chopped fresh coriander
1 tbsp chopped fresh mint
2 tbsps chopped fresh parsley
225g/8oz bulgar wheat
420ml/¾ pint vegetable stock
Mint sprigs, to garnish

Heat the oils in a large saucepan and fry the pepper, onion and pine nuts for 5 minutes. Add the cucumber, herbs and bulgar wheat, then pour in the stock. Bring gently to the boil, stir, cover and simmer gently for 10-15 minutes or until the stock has been absorbed, stirring occasionally. Serve hot or cold garnished with sprigs of mint.

Time: Preparation takes about 10 minutes, cooking takes about 20 minutes.

Serving Idea: Serve with a mixed salad.

Variation: Use brown rice instead of bulgar wheat in this recipe and increase the cooking time accordingly.

Ratatouille Pie with Cheese & — Peanut Pastry —

A colourful dish to make in the autumn when aubergines and courgettes are cheap and plentiful.

SERVES 4-6

Ratatouille
2 tbsps olive oil

2 onions, chopped

4 tomatoes, sliced

1 aubergine, sliced

3 courgettes, finely sliced

2 sticks celery chopped

White sauce
60g/2oz flour

60g/2oz butter or margarine

420ml/¾ pint milk

Pastry
60g/2oz butter

120g/4oz self-raising flour

60g/2oz finely grated vegetarian cheese

60g/2oz salted peanuts, finely chopped

A little milk

Beaten egg to glaze

Put the oil and all the vegetables into a large pan and cook gently for about 20 minutes or until soft. To make the sauce, melt the margarine in a separate pan, stir in the flour and cook for 2 minutes, stirring all the time. Gradually add the milk and bring to boiling point. Stir the sauce into the vegetable mixture and put into an ovenproof dish.

Rub the butter into the flour and add the cheese and peanuts.

Add a little milk and roll out the pastry. Place on top of the ratatouille mixture, trim and brush with beaten egg. Bake in an oven preheated to 190°C/375°F/Gas Mark 5 for about 30 minutes or until golden brown.

Time: Preparation takes 30 minutes, cooking takes 1 hour.

Serving Idea: Serve with bundles of julienne vegetables – carrots, swede, turnips etc.

Variation: Sliced green pepper can be used in place of the celery.

Courgette & Sweetcorn Savoury

This is an excellent way to use up leftover pasta.

SERVES 4

1 tbsp oil

1 medium onion, chopped

225g/8oz courgettes, sliced

200g/7oz can sweetcorn, drained

175g/6oz cooked pasta shapes

Large pinch of dried oregano

1 tbsp tomato purée

Salt and freshly ground black pepper

Sauce

30g/1oz butter or margarine

30g/1oz wholewheat flour

275ml/½ pint skimmed milk

3 tbsps white wine

60g/2oz strong vegetarian cheese, grated

Topping

30g/1oz wholemeal breadcrumbs

2 tsps sunflower seeds

Heat the oil in a frying pan and sauté the chopped onion until soft. Add the sliced courgettes and brown lightly. Mix in the sweetcorn, cooked pasta, oregano and tomato purée, and stir. Season lightly and transfer the mixture to an oiled ovenproof dish.

Make the cheese sauce by melting the margarine and stirring in the flour to make a roux. Heat gently for a few minutes and then pour on the milk and wine, stirring all the time, to make a smooth sauce. Add the grated cheese and stir until it melts into the sauce. Remove from the heat and pour over the vegetable mixture. Top with the breadcrumbs and sunflower seeds. Bake in an oven preheated to 180°C/350°F/Gas Mark 4, for about 20 minutes until the dish is brown and bubbling.

Time: Preparation takes about 30 minutes, cooking takes 20 minutes.

Serving Idea: Serve with grilled tomatoes and creamed potatoes.

Conchiglie with
— Two Sauces —

A very low fat pasta dish with two delicious sauces

SERVES 4

450g/1lb cooked conchiglie (pasta shells)

Tomato sauce

1 large onion, very finely chopped

1 tsp bouillon powder

3 tbsps water

1 clove garlic, crushed

½ tsp dried thyme

Pinch of ground rosemary

400g/14oz tin tomatoes

Mushroom sauce

250g/9oz oyster mushrooms

30g/1oz butter or margarine

1 tsp bouillon powder

4 tbsps fromage frais

Chopped fresh parsley for garnish

To make the tomato sauce, place the onion, bouillon powder, water and garlic in a pan and cook very gently for 7-10 minutes until the onion is soft. Add the thyme and rosemary and cook for 1 minute. Chop the tomatoes and add to the pan together with the tomato juice. Bring to the boil and boil rapidly until the sauce has reduced and thickened.

To make the mushroom sauce, chop the mushrooms finely. Melt the margarine in a pan and add the bouillon powder and mushrooms. Simmer very gently for 10-15 minutes. Remove from the heat and stir in the fromage frais. Heat gently until hot, but do not boil.

Divide the pasta between 4 serving dishes and pour the tomato sauce over one half of the pasta and the mushroom sauce over the other side of the pasta. Sprinkle the chopped parsley between the two sauces. Serve at once.

Time: Preparation takes about 20 minutes, cooking, including the pasta, takes 35 minutes.

Cook's Tip: The sauces may be prepared in advance, refrigerated and reheated when required. Use fresh or dried pasta, but remember that dried pasta takes longer to cook.

Variation: Both sauces are suitable for use on their own – just double the quantities given.

Sweet Bean Curry

This excellent curry will freeze well for up to six weeks.

SERVES 4

175g/6oz red kidney beans, soaked overnight

30g/1oz butter or margarine

1 onion, sliced

1 apple, cored and chopped

175g/6oz mushrooms, sliced

1 tbsp curry powder

30g/1oz plain flour

570ml/1 pint bean stock or bean stock and water

Salt to taste

1 tbsp lemon juice

1 tbsp chutney

60g/2oz sultanas

60g/2oz coconut cream, grated or chopped

Drain the beans, put into a large pan and cover with cold water. Bring to the boil and boil vigorously for 10-15 minutes; turn down the heat and boil for about an hour until the beans are tender but still whole.

Melt the butter or margarine and cook the onion until it is very brown. Add the apple and mushrooms and cook for 2-3 minutes. Add the curry powder and flour and cook for a couple of minutes, stirring all the time. Gradually add the bean stock and stir until smooth. Add the seasoning, lemon juice, chutney, sultanas and beans and cook for 10-15 minutes. Just before serving, add the coconut cream and stir until dissolved.
Time: Preparation takes 25 minutes. Cooking time, including the beans, 1 hour 25 minutes.

Piper's Pie

Accompany this attractive dish with carrots and sweetcorn for the perfect family meal.

SERVES 4

450g/1lb potaotes, peeled and diced

175g/6oz mung beans

225g/8oz leeks

1 onion, sliced

½ tsp dill

2.5cm/1 inch fresh ginger, chopped or finely grated

1 tbsp concentrated apple juice

1 tsp miso

Boil the potatoes and mash with a little butter and seasoning. In a separate pan, cover the mung beans with water and boil for 15-20 minutes until soft.

Meanwhile, generously butter an ovenproof casserole dish and put in the leeks, onion, dill, ginger and concentrated apple juice. Mix well. Drain the beans, reserving the stock, and add to the casserole dish. Dissolve the miso in a little of the bean stock and mix into the casserole which should be moist but not too wet. Cover and cook in an oven preheated to 200°C/400°F/Gas Mark 6 for 30-45 minutes, stirring a couple of times during the cooking and adding a little more bean stock if necessary.

Remove from the oven and cover with a layer of mashed potatoes. Return to the oven to brown, or brown under the grill.
Time: Preparation takes 20 minutes, cooking takes 50-60 minutes.
Variation: A small tin of sweetcorn may be added to the pie before covering with the mashed potatoes.

Vegetarian Spaghetti — Bolognaise —

Any cooked beans can be used in this recipe.

SERVES 2-4

340g/12oz wholewheat spaghetti

60ml/4 tbsps olive oil

225g/8oz onions, chopped

1 clove garlic, crushed

400g/14oz can chopped tomatoes

120g/4oz carrots, diced

2 sticks celery, sliced

120g/4oz mushrooms, sliced

1 small red pepper, diced

½ tsp basil

½ tsp oregano

¼ tsp nutmeg

2 tbsps tomato purée

280ml/½ pint stock or water

175g/6oz cooked aduki beans

2 tsps soya flour

Salt and freshly ground black pepper

Vegetarian parmesan cheese

Cook the spaghetti following the instructions on the packet. Heat the olive oil in a large pan and cook the onions and garlic until browned. Add the tomatoes, carrots, celery, mushrooms, pepper, basil, oregano, nutmeg, tomato purée and stock. Stir well and simmer for about 20 minutes or until the vegetables are cooked. Add the cooked beans and cook for a further 5 minutes.

Mix the soya flour with a little water; add to the sauce and allow to cook for 2 minutes. Season to taste. Drain the spaghetti and serve topped with the Bolognaise sauce and a sprinkling of Parmesan cheese.

Time: Preparation takes about 30 minutes, cooking takes 35 minutes.

Cook's Tip: Add a tablespoon of oil to the water in which the spaghetti is cooked to prevent it from sticking together.

Stuffed Marrow

This makes a nice change from the more common stuffed vegetables.

SERVES 4

1 medium marrow
¾oz/6 tbsps fresh brown breadcrumbs
2-4 tbsps milk
4 eggs, hard boiled
120g/4oz grated cheese
Salt and pepper
Pinch of freshly grated nutmeg
1 egg, beaten
A little margarine or butter
Parsley and 1 red pepper for garnish

Wash the marrow well, cut in half lengthwise and scoop out the seeds. Place in a well greased baking tin or dish. Soak the breadcrumbs in the milk. Chop the hard-boiled eggs and add to the breadcrumbs together with the cheese, seasoning and nutmeg. Bind the mixture with the beaten egg. Pile into the marrow halves and dot with knobs of margarine or butter. Pour a little water around the marrow and bake in an oven preheated to 190°C/375°F/Gas Mark 5 for 35-40 minutes until the marrow is tender and the top is nicely browned. (If the top is browning too quickly, cover with silver foil.) Serve on a large dish garnished with parsley and red pepper rings.
Time: Preparation takes 25 minutes, cooking takes 35-40 minutes.
Serving Idea: For a special occasion garnish with cranberries and surround with sliced red or yellow peppers, chopped lettuce and watercress.

Express Vegetable Pie

Any cooked, leftover vegetables may be used for this quick and easy pie.

SERVES 4

1 large onion, finely chopped
30g/1oz margarine
2 sticks celery, diced
90g/3oz cashew nuts, chopped and dry roasted
675g/1½lbs mixed frozen vegetables (peas, corn, swede, carrot, turnip, diced peppers, parsnip etc.)
2 tsps tomato purée
140ml/¼ pint water or stock
½-1 tsp yeast extract
Salt and freshly ground black pepper
3-4 large potatoes
Knob of butter
A little milk

Sauté the onion in the margarine together with the celery and a little water until just tender. Add the remaining ingredients apart from the potatoes, butter and milk. Simmer for 3-5 minutes, adding a little more water if the mixture seems too dry. Keep hot.

Cook the potatoes until soft; mash with a knob of butter and a little milk, adding salt and pepper to taste. Turn the vegetable mixture into a casserole dish and cover completely with the mashed potato. Fork over the top roughly, dot with butter and grill for 3-5 minutes until golden brown. Serve immediately.
Time: Preparation takes 20 minutes, cooking takes 15 minutes.
Serving Idea: Serve with salad, mushrooms and pumpkin seeds.

Courgettes Mediterranean Style

Any type of cooked bean may be used for this dish.

SERVES 4

3 tbsps olive oil
1 large onion, finely chopped
3 cloves garlic, crushed
1 red pepper, chopped
225g/8oz cooked haricot beans
400g/14oz can tomatoes
450g/1lb courgettes, finely sliced
1 tsp oregano
Salt and freshly ground black pepper

Heat the oil in a pan. Add the onion, garlic and pepper and cook for 4-5 minutes. Add the cooked beans, tinned tomatoes and courgettes. Stir well. Add the oregano and seasoning, and stir again. Cover and cook slowly for 30 minutes.
Time: Preparation takes 10-15 minutes, cooking takes 40 minutes.
Serving Idea: Serve on a bed of white rice.
Cook's Tip: This dish will reheat well.

Speedy Pizza

The perfect meal for cooks in a hurry.

SERVES 4-6

Pastry
225g/8oz wholemeal self-raising flour
90g/3oz vegetarian suet
Scant ½ tsp salt
Cold water to mix, approx. 225ml/8fl oz

Filling
Olive oil
1 tbsp tomato purée
1 medium onion, very finely chopped
400g/14oz can artichokes, halved
6 medium tomatoes, skinned and sliced
1 tsp dried oregano
120g/4oz vegetarian Cheddar cheese, finely sliced
12 black olives, pitted and halved (optional)

Mix the flour, salt and suet together in a large bowl and add enough cold water to make a pliable dough. Roll out into a 25cm/10-inch round and place on a greased baking sheet. Brush with olive oil and cover with the tomato purée. Arrange the onion, artichokes and tomatoes on top. Sprinkle with oregano. Arrange the cheese over the mixture and place the olives on top. Bake in an oven preheated to 190°C/375°F/Gas Mark 5, for about 35 minutes.
Time: Preparation takes 10 minutes, cooking takes 35 minutes.
Serving Idea: Serve with jacket potatoes and a crisp salad.

Pasta Spirals with Walnuts & Stilton

This classic combination of walnuts and Stilton creates an unusual but delicious Italian-style meal.

SERVES 4

450g/1lb pasta spirals
280ml/½ pint double cream
450g/1lb vegetarian Stilton cheese
120g/4oz walnut halves
Salt and freshly ground black pepper
4 sprigs fresh thyme, to garnish
2 ripe figs, to garnish

Cook the pasta in plenty of lightly salted, boiling water for 10 minutes or as directed on the packet. Pour the cream into a saucepan and bring to the boil. Boil rapidly for 3 minutes, then crumble in the Stilton cheese and stir until it melts. Stir in the walnut halves and season with pepper.

When the pasta is cooked, drain well, rinse with boiling water and return to the pan. Pour the cream and cheese sauce onto the pasta and toss well. Garnish with sprigs of thyme and ½ a ripe fig before serving.

Time: Preparation takes about 5 minutes, cooking takes about 20 minutes.

Cook's Tip: The walnut sauce, or either of the variations, make a superb fondue sauce into which can be dipped crusty bread or fresh vegetables.

Cheese Sandwich Soufflé

Unlike a true soufflé, there is no need to rush this dish to the table as it will not sink. It is equally delicious served hot or cold.

SERVES 4

1 tbsp wholegrain mustard
8 slices wholemeal bread
2 tomatoes, sliced
175g/6oz vegetarian Cheddar cheese, grated
2 eggs, beaten
570ml/1 pint milk
1 tsp dried basil
Salt and freshly ground black pepper
Parsley sprigs, to garnish

Preheat the oven to 180°C/350°F/Gas Mark 4. Spread equal amounts of mustard over four slices of the bread. Arrange the tomato slices over the mustard-spread bread and sprinkle with the grated cheese. Use the remaining four slices of bread to cover the cheese. Place the cheese and tomato sandwiches in a large, shallow dish or 4 smaller individual dishes into which they will just fit. Beat together the eggs, milk and basil, and season well. Pour over the bread, allow to stand for 30 minutes to allow the bread to soak up the milk mixture.

Bake for 40-45 minutes or until the milk mixture is set. Serve garnished with sprigs of parsley.

Time: Preparation takes about 10 minutes, plus 30 minutes standing. Cooking takes about 45 minutes.

Vegetarian Paella

This tasty dish is perfect served with crusty bread and a green salad.

SERVES 4-6

60ml/4 tbsps olive oil
1 large onion, chopped
2 cloves garlic, crushed
½ tsp paprika
340g/12oz long-grain brown rice
1.14 litres/1½ pints stock
175ml/6 fl oz dry white wine
400g/14oz can chopped tomatoes
1 tbsp tomato purée
½ tsp tarragon
1 tsp basil
1 tsp oregano
1 red pepper, roughly chopped
1 green pepper, roughly chopped
3 sticks celery, finely chopped
225g/8oz mushrooms, washed and sliced
60g/2oz mange tout, trimmed and halved
120g/4oz frozen peas
60g/2oz cashew nut pieces
Salt and freshly ground black pepper

Heat the oil and fry the onion and garlic until soft. Add the paprika and rice and continue to cook for 4-5 minutes until the rice is transparent. Stir occasionally. Add the stock, wine, tomatoes, tomato purée and herbs and simmer for 10-15 minutes.

Add the pepper, celery, mushrooms and mange tout and continue to cook for another 30 minutes until the rice is cooked. Add the peas, cashew nuts and seasoning to taste. Heat through and place on a large heated serving dish. Sprinkle the parsley over the top and garnish with lemon wedges and olives.

Time: Preparation takes 20 minutes, cooking takes 45 minutes.

Cook's Tip: To prepare in advance, undercook slightly, add a little more stock or water and reheat. Do not add the peas until just before serving otherwise they will lose their colour.

Sweetcorn & Parsnip Flan

Serve this unusual flan with jacket potatoes filled with cottage cheese and chives.

SERVES 6

Base

90g/3oz soft margarine

175g/6oz wholemeal flour

1 tsp baking powder

Pinch of salt

60-90ml/4-6 tbsps ice-cold water

1 tbsp oil

Filling

1 large onion, finely chopped

1 clove garlic, crushed

30g/1oz butter or margarine

2 large parsnips, steamed and roughly mashed

175g/6oz sweetcorn, frozen or canned

1 tsp dried basil

Salt and freshly ground black pepper

3 eggs

140ml/¼ pint milk

90g/3oz grated vegetarian Cheddar cheese

1 medium tomato, sliced

Rub the margarine into the flour, baking powder and salt until the mixture resembles fine breadcrumbs. Add the water and oil and work together lightly. The mixture should be fairly moist. Leave for half an hour. Roll out the pastry and use it to line a 25.4cm/10-inch flan dish. Prick the bottom and bake blind at 210°C/425°F/Gas Mark 7 for about 8 minutes.

Meanwhile, sauté the onion and garlic in the butter or margarine until soft and golden. Add the parsnips, sweetcorn and basil and season to taste.

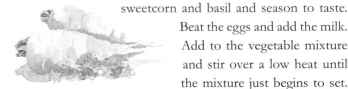

Beat the eggs and add the milk. Add to the vegetable mixture and stir over a low heat until the mixture just begins to set.

Pour into the flan base and top with the grated cheese and sliced tomato. Bake at 190°C/375°F/Gas Mark 5 for 15-20 minutes or until the cheese is golden brown.

Time: Preparation takes about 40 minutes, cooking takes 30 minutes.

Cook's Tip: The partial cooking of the whole mixture before placing in the flan base helps to keep the base from becoming soggy and considerably reduces the cooking time.

Vegetable Stew with Herb — Dumplings —

The ideal meal to warm up a cold winter's night

SERVES 4-6

1 large onion
900g/2lbs mixed vegetables (carrot, swede, parsnips, turnips, cauliflower etc.)
570ml/1 pint vegetable stock
Salt and freshly ground black pepper
Flour or proprietory gravy powder to thicken

Dumplings
120g/4oz wholewheat self-raising flour
60g/2oz vegetarian suet
1 tsp mixed herbs
¼ tsp salt

Chop the onion into large pieces. Peel and prepare the vegetables and chop into bite-sized pieces. Put the onion and vegetables into a pan and cover with the stock. Bring to the boil and simmer for 20 minutes. Season to taste.

Mix a little flour or gravy powder with a little water and stir into the stew to thicken. Place the ingredients for the dumplings into a bowl and add just enough water to bind. Shape the mixture into 8 small dumplings. Bring the stew to the boil and drop in the dumplings. Cover and allow to simmer for 10 minutes. Serve at once.

Time: Preparation takes 10 minutes, cooking takes 30 minutes
Serving Idea: Serve with boiled potatoes.
Variation: The mixed herbs may be omitted when making the dumplings or chopped fresh parsley and a squeeze of lemon juice may be used instead.

Savoury Bean Pot

Serve this exciting mixture with rice or jacket potatoes and a salad.

SERVES 4

2 tbsps vegetable oil
2 vegetable stock cubes, crumbled
2 medium onions, chopped
2 eating apples, peeled and grated
2 medium carrots, grated
3 tbsps tomato purée
280ml/½ pint water
2 tbsps white wine vinegar
1 tbsp mustard powder
1 tsp dried oregano
1 tsp ground cumin
2 tsps brown sugar
Salt and freshly ground black pepper
450g/1lb cooked red kidney beans
A little soured cream

Heat the oil in a non-stick pan. Add the crumbled stock cubes, onions, apples and carrots. Sauté for 5 minutes, stirring continuously. Mix the tomato purée with the water and add together with all the other ingredients apart from the beans and cream. Stir well, cover and simmer for 2 minutes. Add the beans and tip the mixture into an ovenproof casserole. Cover and cook in an oven preheated to 180°C/350°F/Gas Mark 4, for 35-40 minutes. Add a little more water after 20 minutes if necessary. Top with swirls of soured cream and serve.

Time: Preparation takes 20 minutes, cooking takes 45 minutes.

Tofu Spinach Flan

Serve this tasty flan with a medley of lightly cooked fresh vegetables.

SERVES 4

Pastry

1 tsp brown sugar

2-3 tbsps water

2 tsps oil

120g/4oz wholemeal flour

½ tsp baking powder

Pinch of salt

60g/2oz butter or hard margarine

Filling

225g/8oz spinach

275g/10oz tofu

Juice of 1 lemon

2 tbsps shoyu sauce (Japanese soy sauce)

60ml/4 tbsps sunflower oil

140ml/¼ pint soya milk

Salt according to taste

175g/6oz onions, chopped

Dissolve the sugar in the water and mix in the oil. Keep cool. Mix the flour, baking powder and salt together in a large bowl. Rub in the margarine until the mixture resembles fine breadcrumbs. Add the fluid mixture and mix into the flour, using more water if necessary. The dough should be of a wettish consistency. Leave to rest under the upturned bowl for half an hour.

Roll out the dough to line an 18-20cm/7-8-inch flan dish. Line the dish and bake blind for 5-6 minutes.

Wash the spinach, drain and cook in its own juices in a covered pan until soft – about 5-8 minutes. Drain the spinach, chop and set aside. Crumble the tofu into a blender, add the lemon juice, shoyu, 2 tbsps of the oil, the soya milk and salt. Blend to a thick creamy consistency. Adjust the seasoning if necessary. Chop the onions and fry them in the remaining oil until lightly browned. Add the spinach and fold in the tofu cream. Pour the mixture into the prepared flan shell and bake in the middle of an oven preheated to 190°C/375°F/Gas Mark 5, for 30 minutes or until set. Allow to cool for about 10 minutes before serving.

Time: Preparation takes 25 minutes, cooking takes 45 minutes.

Watchpoint: The filling may develop cracks on cooling but this is normal.

Lentil Moussaka

Try a taste of the Greek Islands with this classic dish.

SERVES 4-6

150g/5oz green lentils

1 large aubergine, sliced

60-75ml/4-5 tbsps oil

1 large onion, chopped

1 clove garlic, crushed

1 large carrot, diced

4 sticks celery, finely chopped

1-2 tsps mixed herbs

400g/14oz can tomatoes

2 tsps shoyu sauce (Japanese soy sauce)

Freshly ground black pepper

2 medium potatoes, cooked and sliced

2 large tomatoes, sliced

Sauce

60g/2oz butter or margarine

60g/2oz brown rice flour

420ml/³/₄ pint milk

1 large egg, separated

60g/2oz grated vegetarian Cheddar cheese

1 tsp grated nutmeg

Cook the lentils in plenty of water until soft. Drain and reserve the liquid. Fry the aubergine in the oil, drain well and set aside. Sauté the onion, garlic, carrot, celery and a little of the lentil stock. Simmer with the lid on until just tender. Add the lentils, mixed herbs and tinned tomatoes. Simmer gently for 3-4 minutes. Season with the shoyu and pepper. Place a layer of the lentil mixture in a large casserole dish and cover with half of the aubergine slices. Cover the aubergine slices with half of the potato slices and all the tomato. Repeat with the remaining lentils, aubergines and potatoes. To make the sauce, melt the margarine in a saucepan, remove from the heat and stir in the flour to make a roux. Add the milk gradually, blending well, so that the sauce is smooth and lump free. Return to the heat and stir continually until the sauce thickens. Remove the pan from the heat and cool slightly. Add the egg yolk, stir in the cheese and add the nutmeg.

Beat the egg white until it is stiff, then carefully fold into the sauce. Pour the sauce over the moussaka, covering the dish completely. Bake in an oven preheated to 180°C/350°F/Gas Mark 4, for about 40 minutes until the top is golden brown and puffy.

Time: Preparation takes 45 minutes, cooking takes 1 hour 10 minutes.

Freezing: Assemble the mixture without the sauce and freeze. Defrost, add the sauce and cook from the point of beating in the egg white.

Serving Idea: Serve with a crunchy green salad or battered mushrooms.

Fifteen Minute Goulash

This quick and easy goulash is best served with baked potatoes.

SERVES 4

1 onion, finely chopped

1 clove garlic, crushed

2 carrots, diced

3 medium courgettes, diced

2 tbsps olive oil

1 tbsp paprika

Pinch of nutmeg

1 heaped tbsp freshly chopped parsley

1 tbsp tomato purée

400g/14oz can tomatoes

225g/8oz cooked red kidney beans or 14oz can, drained and washed

140ml/¼ pint tomato juice or stock

Salt and freshly groundpepper

Soured cream or yogurt to serve

Put the onion, garlic, carrots and courgettes into a pan with the olive oil and sauté for 5 minutes until softened. Stir in the paprika, nutmeg, parsley and tomato purée. Add the rest of the ingredients except cream or yogurt and cook over a low heat for 10 minutes.

Turn onto a hot serving dish and top with a little soured cream or yogurt.

Time: Preparation takes 10 minutes, cooking takes 15 minutes.

Variation: Vary the type of bean used – try haricots, soya beans or chickpeas.

Mushroom Stroganoff

A great favourite which is much appreciated by all age groups.

SERVES 4

2 medium onions, sliced

5 sticks celery, chopped

60g/2oz butter or margarine

450g/1lb tiny button mushrooms

½ tsp mixed herbs

½ tsp basil

1 large heaped tbsp plain flour

280ml/½ pint vegetable stock

Salt and freshly ground black pepper

75ml/2½fl oz soured cream or yogurt

Chopped fresh parsley

Put the onions and celery into a large pan together with the butter or margarine and sauté over a low heat until the onions are transparent. Add the mushrooms and cook for 2-3 minutes until the juices run. Add the mixed herbs and basil. Stir in the flour and cook for 1 minute. Add the stock and seasoning and allow to cook gently for 8-10 minutes.

Remove from the heat, stir in the soured cream and adjust the seasoning if necessary. Heat very gently to serving temperature but do not allow to boil. Garnish with the chopped parsley and serve at once.

Time: Preparation takes 10 minutes, cooking takes 20 minutes.

Serving Idea: Serve on a bed of Walnut Rice – cook enough rice to serve 4-6 people and carefully fold in seasoning, a little butter, 1 crushed clove of garlic and 60g/2oz finely chopped walnuts.

Green Lentils with Fresh Ginger & Spices

There's certainly no lack of taste in this spicy lentil mix.

SERVES 4

175g/6oz green lentils

Water or stock to cover

30g/1oz margarine or 1 tbsp soya or sunflower oil

1 medium onion, finely chopped

2.5cm/1-inch piece fresh root ginger, peeled and grated

1 tsp garam masala

1 tsp cumin seeds

1 tsp coriander seeds, crushed

1 tsp green cardamom pods, seeds removed and crushed

1 medium carrot, scrubbed and diced

400g/14oz can peeled Italian tomatoes

60g/2oz mushrooms, cleaned and finely chopped

1 tbsp shoyu sauce (Japanese soy sauce)

1 tbsp cider vinegar

Salt and freshly ground black pepper to taste

Chopped fresh parsley or coriander to garnish

Pick over the lentils and wash thoroughly. Place in a large, heavy-based saucepan, cover with water or stock and bring to the boil. Turn off the heat, cover and leave to begin to swell.

Meanwhile, heat the margarine or oil in a separate saucepan and gently fry the onion, ginger and spices until they are well combined, softening and giving off a tempting aroma. Add to the lentils, bring to the boil and start to add the other vegetables, allowing several minutes between each addition, beginning with the carrot followed by the tomatoes and lastly the chopped mushrooms. Stir frequently to prevent sticking and check on liquid quantity regularly, adding more water or stock as necessary. Just before the end of the cooking time – approximately 25 minutes depending on the age of the lentils – add the shoyu, cider vinegar and salt and pepper. Cook for a few more minutes and serve hot garnished with slices of lemon and freshly chopped parsley or coriander.

Time: Preparation takes about 25 minutes, cooking takes about 45 minutes.

Serving Idea: Serve with boiled brown rice or jacket potatoes and a salad made from beansprouts, red and green peppers and grated daikon.

Variation: Black olives can replace the chopped parsley or coriander.

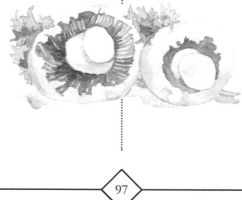

Cheese & Tomato Pasta

This favourite Italian classic is perfect served as a lunch or supper dish and will be popular with all the family.

225g/8oz tagliatelle verdi

1 tbsp vegetable oil

1 onion, chopped

120g/4oz mushrooms, finely sliced

1 tbsp tomato purée

400g/14oz can chopped tomatoes

2 tbsps dried mixed herbs

120g/4oz vegetarian Cheddar cheese, grated

Salt and freshly ground black pepper

Cook the pasta in plenty of lightly salted, boiling water for 10 minutes or as directed on the packet. Meanwhile, heat the oil in a frying pan and sauté the onion until beginning to soften. Add the mushrooms and fry for 3 minutes. Stir in the tomato purée, tomatoes and herbs and simmer gently while the pasta cooks.

When the pasta is cooked, stir most of the cheese into the tomato sauce. Season. Drain the pasta and pile onto a serving dish. Spoon the sauce into the centre and top with the remaining cheese.

Time: Preparation takes about 10 minutes, cooking takes about 20 minutes.

Serving Idea: Serve with a mixed Italian salad and hot garlic bread.

Variation: Use any variety of pasta shapes in this recipe.

Cook's Tip: Fresh pasta is now readily available and very quick to cook. You will need about twice the weight of dried pasta.

Savoury Grain Casserole

Serve as a complete meal for 2 people or serve accompanied with lightly steamed vegetables for 4 people.

SERVES 2-4

90g/3oz brown rice

90g/3oz split peas

2 sticks celery, very finely chopped

1 medium onion, very finely chopped

120g/4oz mushrooms, chopped

400g/14oz can tomatoes, drained and chopped or

225g/8oz tomatoes, skinned and chopped

½ tsp dill seeds

½ tsp thyme

2 tbsps shoyu sauce (Japanese soy sauce)

1 egg, beaten

120g/4oz vegetarian Cheddar cheese, grated

Cover the rice with water and cook for 10-15 minutes, then drain. Cover the split peas with water and cook for 20 minutes until just tender but not mushy, then drain. Meanwhile, combine the celery, onion, mushrooms, tomatoes, dill, thyme, shoyu and the egg in a large bowl. Stir in the rice and peas. Place the mixture in a greased ovenproof casserole dish and bake in an oven preheated to 180°C/350°F/Gas Mark 4, for 45 minutes. Remove from the oven and sprinkle with the grated cheese. Return to the oven for 10 minutes until the cheese has melted. Serve at once.

Time: Preparation takes 10 minutes, cooking takes 1 hour 45 minutes.

Cabbage Parcels

The nutty texture and flavour of these filled cabbage leaves is ideally complemented by the mushroom and tomato sauce.

120g/4oz soup pasta

8-12 large cabbage leaves, washed

1 hard-boiled egg, finely chopped

60g/2oz walnuts, chopped

1 tbsp chopped fresh chives

2 tbsps fresh chopped parsley

1 tsp fresh chopped marjoram

Salt and freshly ground black pepper

280ml/½ pint vegetable stock

1 tbsp walnut oil

1 onion, finely chopped

1 green pepper, chopped

400g/14oz can chopped tomatoes

120g/4oz button mushrooms, chopped

2 tbsps tomato purée

1 bay leaf

Pinch of sugar

Cook the pasta in plenty of lightly salted, boiling water for 8 minutes or as directed on the packet. Remove the thick stems from the base of the cabbage leaves and then blanch the leaves in boiling water for 3 minutes, drain and refresh in cold water.

When the pasta is cooked, drain well and mix with the egg, walnuts and herbs, and season. Divide the pasta mixture between the cabbage leaves, fold up to enclose the filling completely and secure with cocktail sticks. Place in a shallow, ovenproof casserole dish and add the stock. Cover and bake in an oven preheated to 180°C/350°F/Gas Mark 4, for 40 minutes.

Heat the oil in a frying pan and fry the onion and pepper for 5 minutes or until soft. Stir in the remaining ingredients, season, and cook gently for 10 minutes. Remove the cabbage parcels from the casserole dish with a draining spoon and serve with the sauce poured over them.

Time: Preparation takes about 30 minutes, cooking takes about 1 hour.

Vegetable Couscous

Couscous is a popular dish in North Africa, where it is often cooked by steaming over an accompanying stew.

SERVES 4

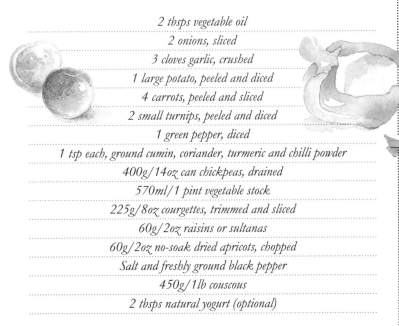

2 tbsps vegetable oil

2 onions, sliced

3 cloves garlic, crushed

1 large potato, peeled and diced

4 carrots, peeled and sliced

2 small turnips, peeled and diced

1 green pepper, diced

1 tsp each, ground cumin, coriander, turmeric and chilli powder

400g/14oz can chickpeas, drained

570ml/1 pint vegetable stock

225g/8oz courgettes, trimmed and sliced

60g/2oz raisins or sultanas

60g/2oz no-soak dried apricots, chopped

Salt and freshly ground black pepper

450g/1lb couscous

2 tbsps natural yogurt (optional)

Heat the oil in a large saucepan and fry the onions until beginning to soften. Add the garlic, potato, carrots, turnips and green pepper and sauté for 5 minutes. Stir in the spices and cook for 1 minute. Add the chickpeas, stock, courgettes, raisins or sultanas and apricots. Season with salt and pepper. Bring gently to the boil and simmer for 30 minutes.

Meanwhile, place the couscous in a large bowl and cover with boiling water. Allow to stand for 15 minutes, then place in a steamer lined with muslin and steam for 15 minutes.

Pile the couscous onto a serving place and serve the vegetables on top. Garnish with a little yogurt if wished.

Time: Preparation takes about 20 minutes, cooking takes about 40 minutes.

Preparation: The couscous can be placed in a steamer and steamed on top of the vegetables if wished.

Butter Beans in Tomato Sauce

A tasty tomato sauce perfectly complements the beans in this easy recipe.

SERVES 4-6

175g/6oz butter beans, soaked overnight
60g/2oz butter or margarine
1 onion, sliced
6 medium tomatoes, sliced
60g/2oz flour
1 bay leaf
A little milk
Salt and freshly ground black pepper
Chopped fresh parsley

Drain the butter beans and put into a pan with fresh water to cover; cook slowly until soft. Melt the butter or margarine and cook the onions with the tomatoes and bay leaf until soft. Stir in the flour, and add a little cooking water from the beans to make a thick sauce. Stir well and add a little milk and seasoning to taste. Remove the bay leaf and pour the sauce over the beans. Sprinkle with the chopped parsley.

Time: Preparation takes 20 minutes. Cooking time, including the beans, 1½-1¾ hours.

Serving Idea: Serve with baked potatoes and lightly cooked vegetables.

Cook's Tip: When cold, this savoury can be mashed to make a sandwich paste or for use with a mixed salad. Any leftovers can be used as a basis for soup.

Butter Bean One-Pot

This is a quickly prepared, all-in-one supper dish.

SERVES 4

2 tbsps vegetable oil
1 green pepper, finely chopped
1 large onion, finely chopped
2 sticks celery, diced
400g/14oz can tomatoes
2 large potatoes, peeled and diced
280ml/½ pint vegetable stock or water
2 tbsps finely chopped parsley
Salt and freshly ground black pepper
450g/1lb cooked butter beans

Put the oil, pepper, onion and celery into a pan and cook gently until the onion begins to brown. Add the tomatoes and their juice, plus the potatoes, stock, parsley, salt and pepper. Simmer for about 30 minutes or until the liquid is reduced by half. Add the beans and heat through gently for 5-10 minutes.

Time: Preparation takes about 15 minutes, cooking takes 50 minutes.

Serving Idea: Serve with lots of crusty bread. Garlic bread also goes well with this dish.

Variation: To make a more substantial main course dish, after adding the beans, stir well and place in a casserole dish. Top with a crumble mixture and bake in a hot oven for 25 minutes.

Lentil Savoury

This dish is quick and easy to prepare and very nutritious.

SERVES 4

175g/6oz lentils
½ tsp basil
½ tsp mixed herbs
2 medium onions, chopped
60g/2oz butter or margarine
2 tbsps tomato purée
400g/14oz can tomatoes
1 tsp brown sugar
Salt and freshly ground black pepper
175g/6oz vegetarian Cheddar cheese, sliced
140ml/¼ pint soured cream

Soak the lentils overnight. Add the lentils to a saucepan with the soaking liquid. Add the herbs and simmer with the lentils until tender. Sauté the onion in the fat until soft. Add the lentils and all the other ingredients apart from cheese and cream. Simmer for 15 minutes until thickened and pour into a greased ovenproof dish. Cover with the cheese and cream and grill, or bake in an oven preheated to 180°C/350°F/Gas Mark 4, until the cheese has melted.

Time: Preparation takes 15 minutes, cooking takes 35-45 minutes.

Cook's Tip: The soured cream can be served separately if desired.

Serving Idea: Serve hot with a mixed salad.

Freezing: This lentil savoury will freeze well but do not cover it with cream and cheese until you are reheating it.

Chestnut Hot-Pot

This enticing hot-pot is perfect served with a lightly cooked green vegetable.

SERVES 4-6

675g/1½lbs potatoes
3 medium onions
225g/8oz brown lentils
225g/8oz chestnuts
Salt and freshly ground black pepper
2 tsps yeast extract
420ml/¾ pint warm water
60g/2oz butter or margarine

Peel and slice the potatoes and onions thinly. Put layers of potatoes, onions, lentils and chestnuts into a greased pie dish; ending with a layer of potatoes. Season well between each layer. Dissolve the yeast extract in the warm water and pour over.

Dot with margarine and cover. Bake in an oven preheated to 190°C/350°F/Gas Mark 4, for an hour or until the potatoes are tender. Turn up the oven to 200°C/400°F/Gas Mark 6, remove the lid from the casserole and return to the oven for 10-15 minutes until the potatoes are crispy and golden brown.

Time: Preparation takes 20 minutes, cooking takes 1 hour 15 minutes.

Variation: Dried chestnuts may be used but need to be soaked overnight in stock or water.

Nutty Spaghetti

An easy-to-make lunch or supper dish.

SERVES 4

225g/8oz spaghetti
700ml/1¼ pints boiling, salted water
1 onion, finely chopped
2 tbsps sunflower oil
2½ tsps curry powder
175ml/6fl oz tomato juice
3 tbsps crunchy peanut butter
1 tbsp lemon juice
Lemon twists and peanuts for garnish

Boil the spaghetti until just tender and drain well. Fry the onion in the oil until golden brown. Stir in the curry powder, tomato juice, peanut butter and lemon juice. Simmer for 5 minutes and then stir into the spaghetti.
Time: Preparation takes about 10 minutes, cooking takes 25 minutes.
Serving Idea: Serve garnished with lemon twists and peanuts.
Variation: Almond butter and blanched almonds can be used in place of the peanut butter and peanuts.

Spicy Black-Eyed Beans

A spicy dish from the West Indies.

SERVES 4

225g/8oz black-eyed beans, soaked and cooked.
60ml/4 tbsps vegetable oil
1 large onion, finely chopped
2 cloves garlic, crushed
1 tsp ground cinnamon
½ tsp ground cumin
Salt and freshly ground black pepper
140ml/5fl oz/¼ pint bean stock or water
2 tbsps tomato purée
1 tbsp shoyu sauce (Japanese soy sauce)
2 large tomatoes, skinned and chopped
1 tbsp chopped parsley

Drain the beans well and retain the cooking liquid. Heat the oil and fry the onion and garlic for 4-5 minutes until soft. Stir in the cinnamon, cumin and seasoning and cook for a further 2 minutes. Add the beans, bean stock, tomato purée, shoyu sauce and tomatoes. Stir and bring to the boil. Simmer for 15-20 minutes until thick. Check the seasoning. Serve sprinkled with chopped parsley.
Time: Preparation takes 20 minutes. Cooking time, including the beans, 1 hour 35 minutes.
Serving Idea: Serve over cooked pasta or rice.
Variation: Haricot beans can be used in place of black-eyed beans.

Indian Vegetable Curry

A wonderfully tasty curry which has the added advantage of freezing well.

SERVES 4

Spices

2 tsps turmeric

1 tsp cumin seeds

1 tsp mustard seed

1 tsp fenugreek

4 tsps coriander seeds

½ tsp chilli powder

1 tsp chopped fresh root ginger

1 tsp black peppercorns

1lb onions, finely chopped

Ghee or vegetable oil

280ml/½ pint sterilised milk

2 tbsps white wine vinegar

400g/1 x 14oz tin tomatoes, liquidised with their juice.

1 tbsp tomato purée

2 tsps brown sugar

1 tsp vegetable stock cube dissolved in a little boiling water

900g/2lbs chopped mushrooms or mixed vegetables

(e.g. mushrooms, cauliflower, carrots, potatoes, okra)

Grind all the spices together – this amount will make 3 tbsps of curry powder. Fry the onions in the ghee or vegetable oil until golden. Add the ground spices, lower the heat and cook for 3 minutes, stirring all the time. Add the milk and vinegar and stir well. Add the liquidised tomatoes, tomato purée, sugar and stock.

Bring to the boil, cover and simmer very gently for 1 hour. Add the vegetables and cook until tender – about 30 minutes.

Time: Preparation takes 30 minutes, cooking takes 1 hour 30 minutes.

Serving Idea: Serve with boiled brown rice, chappatis and Cucumber Raita. Cucumber Raita – combine diced cucumber with yogurt, a little chopped mint, a pinch of chilli powder, cumin and seasoning to taste.

Freezing: The curry sauce will freeze well for up to 3 months; so it is well worth while making double the quantity.

Chana Masala

An excellent dish to serve hot as a main course or cold as an accompaniment to a nut loaf.

SERVES 4

1 large onion, chopped

4 cloves garlic, crushed

2.5cm/³⁄₄ inch fresh root ginger, peeled and finely chopped

3 tbsps ghee

1 tbsp ground coriander

2 tsps cumin seed

¹⁄₄ tsp cayenne pepper

1 tsp turmeric

2 tsps roasted cumin seed, ground

1 tbsp amchur (dried mango powder) or 1 tbsp lemon juice

2 tsps paprika

400g/14oz can Italian tomatoes

675g/1¹⁄₂lbs cooked chickpeas (340g/12oz uncooked)

1 tsp garam masala

¹⁄₂ tsp salt

1 fresh green chilli, finely chopped

Sauté the onion, garlic and ginger in the ghee until soft. Add all the spices and fry over a low heat for 1-2 minutes stirring all the time. Add the tomatoes, roughly chopped, together with their juice. Add the cooked chickpeas. Cook for 30 minutes over a medium heat. Add the garam masala, salt and chilli, stir well and serve.

Time: Preparation takes about 15 minutes, cooking takes 30 minutes.

Chickpea Burgers

These burgers are nice cold and are useful for a packed lunch or picnic.

SERVES 4

450g/1lb cooked chickpeas or 2 x 400g/14oz cans chickpeas

1 onion, finely chopped

2 cloves garlic, crushed

2 medium potatoes, cooked and mashed

2 tbsps shoyu sauce (Japanese soy sauce)

2 tsps lemon juice

Freshly ground black pepper

Wholewheat flour

Oil for frying

Put the chickpeas into a large bowl and mash well. Add the onion, garlic, potato, shoyu, lemon juice and pepper. Mix together well. With floured hands, shape heaped tablespoonfuls of the mixture into small burgers. Coat each burger with flour and refrigerate for 1 hour. Heat a little oil and gently fry the burgers on each side until golden brown.

Time: Preparation takes 15 minutes, cooking takes about 15 minutes.

Serving Idea: Serve with a hot, spicy tomato sauce.

Freezing: Cook and freeze for up to 2 months.

Winter Crumble

A variety of hearty vegetables topped with oats and cheese
makes the perfect winter meal.

SERVES 4-6

Topping

90g/3oz butter or margarine
120g/4oz wholewheat flour
60g/2oz rolled oats
120g/4oz vegetarian Cheddar cheese, grated
¼ tsp salt
175ml/6fl oz vegetable stock
280ml/½ pint sweet cider
1 tsp brown sugar
2 carrots, chopped
2 large parsnips, cut into rings
2 sticks celery, chopped
2 heads broccoli, cut into florets
¼ cauliflower, cut into florets
2 tsps wholewheat flour
2 tbsps chopped fresh parsley
1 medium onion, chopped and fried until golden
4 large tomatoes, skinned and sliced
225g/8oz cooked black-eyed beans
Salt and freshly ground black pepper

Make the topping by rubbing the butter into the flour and oats until the mixture resembles fine breadcrumbs. Stir in the cheese and salt. Mix the stock with the cider and sugar and put into a large pan with the carrots and parsnips. Cook until just tender, remove the vegetables and put aside. Add the celery, broccoli and cauliflower to the pan, cook until tender, remove and reserve with other vegetables.

Mix the flour with a little water, add to the cider and cook until thickened, stirring all the time. Cook for 2-3 minutes, remove from the heat and add the parsley. Place the onions, vegetables, tomatoes and beans in a greased casserole and season well. Pour the sauce over the mixture. Sprinkle the topping over and press down a little. Cook in an oven preheated to 200°C/400°F/Gas Mark 6, for 30-35 minutes or until the topping is golden brown.

Time: Preparation takes 20 minutes, cooking takes 1 hour 5 minutes.

Serving Idea: Serve with roast potatoes.

Cook's Tip: The casserole can be prepared in advance. Refrigerate until ready to cook.

Beans Bourguignonne

Rich and flavoursome, this vegetarian adaptation of the traditional French dish makes a luxurious main course when entertaining.

SERVES 4

225g/8oz borlotti or red kidney beans, soaked overnight

1 bay leaf

60ml/4 tbsps olive or vegetable oil

225g/8oz shallots or baby onions, peeled

1 clove garlic, crushed

4 carrots, peeled and cut into 2.5cm/1-inch chunks

225g/8oz button mushrooms

140ml/¼ pint vegetable stock

280ml/½ pint red wine

1 tsp chopped fresh thyme

2 tsps chopped fresh parsley

Salt and freshly ground black pepper

4 slices wholemeal bread, crusts removed

30g/1oz butter or vegetable margarine

Chopped parsley, to garnish

Drain the soaked beans, place in a saucepan with the bay leaf and enough water to cover by 2.5cm/1 inch and bring to the boil. Boil rapidly for 10 minutes. Reduce the heat and cook for 2-3 hours or until the beans are very soft. Drain.

Heat half the oil in a frying pan and fry the shallots or onions, garlic and carrots for 5 minutes. Stir in the mushrooms and fry for 3-4 minutes. Transfer to an ovenproof casserole. Put the stock and wine in a pan and bring to the boil. Boil rapidly for 2-3 minutes, then pour over the vegetables. Stir the beans and herbs into the casserole and season well. Cook in an oven preheated to 190°C/375°F/Gas Mark 5, for 40 minutes.

Just before the end of the cooking time, cut the bread into triangles. Heat the remaining oil with the butter or margarine and fry the bread until golden. Serve the casserole garnished with the bread triangles and a sprinkling of chopped fresh parsley.

Time: Preparation takes about 25 minutes, plus overnight soaking. Cooking takes about 3½ hours.

Asparagus and Olive Quiche

An interesting combination which gives a new twist to a classic dish.

MAKES 2 x 25cm/10-inch QUICHES

2 x 25cm/10-inch part-baked pastry cases
6 eggs
570ml/1 pint single cream
1 tsp salt
Pinch of nutmeg
Salt and freshly ground black pepper
2 tbsps flour
2 cans green asparagus tips
175g/6oz green olives
2 onions, finely chopped and sautéed in a little butter until soft
90g/3oz vegetarian Cheddar cheese, grated
2 tbsps vegetarian Parmesan cheese
60g/2oz butter

Whisk the eggs with the cream. Add the salt, nutmeg and seasoning. Mix a little of the mixture with the flour until smooth, then add to the cream mixture. Arrange the asparagus tips, olives and onion in the pastry shells and pour the cream mixture over the top. Sprinkle with the grated Cheddar and Parmesan. Dot with the butter and bake in an oven preheated to 190°C/375°F/Gas Mark 5, for 25 minutes. Turn down the oven to 180°C/350°F/Gas Mark 4 for a further 15 minutes until the quiches are golden.
Time: Preparation takes 20 minutes, cooking takes 40 minutes.

Sweet Potato & French Bean Pasties

These pasties are a tasty addition to any lunch box or picnic basket.

SERVES 4

225g/8oz wholemeal shortcrust pastry
½ medium onion, finely chopped
1 clove garlic, crushed
1 tbsp oil
½ tsp grated fresh root ginger
¼-½ tsp chilli powder
¼ tsp ground turmeric
½ tsp ground cumin
1 tsp ground coriander
¼ tsp mustard powder
1 medium sweet potato, cooked and finely diced
120g/4oz French beans, chopped into 1.5cm/½-inch lengths
2 tbsps water or stock
Salt and freshly ground black pepper

Fry the onion and garlic in the oil until soft. Add the ginger and all the spices and stir. Add the diced potato, beans and water or stock and cook gently for 4-5 minutes or until the beans begin to cook. Allow the mixture to cool, then season well. Roll out the pastry into 4 circles. Place a quarter of the filling in the centre of each circle and dampen the edges of the pastry with a little water. Join the pastry together over the filling. Make a small hole in each pasty and glaze with milk or egg. Bake in an oven preheated to 200°C/400°F/Gas Mark 6, for 10-15 minutes.
Time: Preparation, including making the pastry, takes 25 minutes. Cooking takes 15-20 minutes.

Beany Lasagne

This tasty lasagne is suitable for a family meal or entertaining friends.

SERVES 4-6

8 strips wholewheat lasagne

1 large onion, finely chopped

1 tbsp vegetable oil

1-2 cloves garlic, crushed

225g/8oz cooked aduki beans

1 green pepper, chopped

400g/11oz can chopped tomatoes

1 tbsp tomato purée

1 tsp dried basil

1 tsp dried oregano

Shoyu sauce (Japanese soy sauce) or salt

Freshly ground black pepper

Sauce

30g/1oz butter or margarine

30g/1oz plain wholewheat flour

400ml/¾ pint milk or soya milk

60g/2oz vegetarian Cheddar cheese, grated (optional)

Salt and freshly ground black pepper

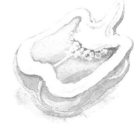

Cook the lasagne in a large pan of boiling, salted water for 8-10 minutes until 'al-dente'. Drain well and drape over a cooling rack or the sides of a colander to cool and prevent sticking together. Soften the onion in a little oil, sprinkling with a little salt to draw out the juice. Add the crushed garlic, beans, green pepper, chopped tomatoes, tomato purée and herbs.

Simmer for about 10 minutes or until the vegetables are tender. Add shoyu sauce and season to taste.

To make the sauce, combine the margarine, flour and cold milk. Gradually bring to the boil, stirring continuously. When thickened, allow to simmer, partly covered, for approximately 6 minutes. Stir the cheese into the sauce and season. Layer the lasagne in a greased dish in the following order: half the bean mix, half the pasta, rest of the bean mix, rest of the pasta, and top with the cheese sauce.

Bake in an oven preheated to 180°C/350°F/Gas Mark 4 for 35 minutes or until golden brown and bubbling. Serve in the dish in which it has been cooked.

Time: Preparation takes 20 minutes, cooking takes about 60 minutes.

Serving Idea: Serve with a green salad.

Cook's Tip: Pre-cooked lasagne can be used but it is important to add an extra amount of liquid to the dish in order to allow the pasta to absorb enough fluid while cooking.

Bulgar Rissotto

This makes a quick lunch dish and is particularly handy if unexpected guests call.

SERVES 3-4

120g/4oz bulgar wheat
1 medium onion, finely chopped
2 sticks celery, finely chopped
1-2 cloves garlic, crushed
15g/¹⁄₂oz butter
1 small red pepper, diced
1 small green pepper, diced
¹⁄₂ tsp dried mixed herbs
60g/2oz peanuts, chopped
1 tsp vegetable extract dissolved in 120ml/4fl oz boiling water
2 tsps shoyu sauce (Japanese soy sauce)
90g/3oz sweetcorn
90g/3oz peas
Salt and freshly ground black pepper
Juice of ¹⁄₂ a lemon

Put the bulgar wheat into a bowl and cover with boiling water. Leave for about 10 minutes after which time the water will have been absorbed and the wheat swollen. Meanwhile, place the onion, celery and garlic into a saucepan and sauté for a few minutes in the butter. Add the peppers, herbs, nuts and vegetable extract. Simmer over a low heat for about 8 minutes. Add the bulgar wheat,

shoyu, sweetcorn, peas and seasoning and mix together well. Continue cooking for a further 5 minutes.

Mix in the lemon juice and transfer to a heated serving dish. Serve immediately.

Time: Preparation takes 15 minutes, cooking takes 20 minutes.

Serving Idea: Serve with a crisp green salad.

Watchpoint: If the risotto is too dry, add a little more water or stock.

Deep Mushroom Pie

A delicious pie and so adaptable. Serve with salad or potatoes and a green vegetable.

SERVES 4

Filling

1 tbsp vegetable oil

340g/¾lb mushrooms, cleaned and chopped

225g/8oz mixed nuts, finely milled

2 medium onions, finely chopped

120g/4oz wholewheat breadcrumbs

2 eggs, beaten

1 tsp dried thyme or 2 tsps fresh chopped

1 tsp dried marjoram or 2 tsps fresh chopped

1 tbsps shoyu (Japanese soy sauce)

Salt and freshly ground black pepper to taste

Small quantity of stock to achieve right consistency if necessary

Pastry

340g/12oz wholewheat flour

Pinch of salt

1 tsp baking powder (optional)

120g/4oz solid vegetable fat

120ml/4fl oz water plus extra boiling water as necessary

Beaten egg to glaze

Heat the oil in a large saucepan and gently fry the onion until soft. Add the finely chopped mushrooms and cook until the juices begin to run. Remove from the heat and add all the other filling ingredients to form a thick but not dry consistency, adding a little stock or water if necessary. Allow to cool.

To prepare the pastry, first sift the flour, salt and baking powder into a large mixing bowl. Cut the fat into small pieces and melt in a saucepan. Add the cold water and bring to a fierce, bubbling boil. Immediately pour into the centre of the flour and mix vigorously with a wooden spoon until glossy. When the mixture is cool enough to handle, use hands and knead it into a ball. Divide the mixture into two-thirds and one-third, placing the one-third portion in an oiled plastic bag to prevent drying out. Use the two-thirds portion to line the base and sides of a 19cm/7-inch spring mould, pressing it down and moulding it into position. Spoon in the mushroom filling and press down firmly making a dome shape. Roll out the remaining pastry to just larger than the tin and place on top of the pie, pinching the edges together to seal.

Trim off any excess pastry and glaze generously with beaten egg. Cut or prick vents in the lid to allow the steam to escape. Bake in an oven preheated to 220°C/425°F/Gas Mark 7, for 20 minutes. Reduce to 190°C/375°F/Gas Mark 5 and bake for a further hour.

Unmould and serve on an attractive platter surrounded by watercress and twists of lemon and cucumber.

Time: Preparation takes about 35 minutes, cooking takes 1 hour 20 minutes.

Stuffed Aubergines

When filled with this delicious stuffing, these interesting vegetables make a substantial hot meal.

SERVES 2

2 large aubergines

2 tbsps vegetable oil

1 onion, chopped

1 clove garlic, crushed

1 green pepper, chopped

60g/2oz mushrooms, chopped

400g/14oz can chopped tomatoes

1 tbsp tomato purée

2 tsps chopped fresh basil

Pinch of sugar

Salt and freshly ground black pepper

30g/1oz wholemeal breadcrumbs

½ tsp dried oregano

30g/1oz walnuts, chopped and lightly toasted

60g/2oz vegetarian Cheddar cheese, grated (optional)

Salad garnish, to serve

Cut the aubergines in half and score the flesh in a criss-cross pattern with a sharp knife. Sprinkle liberally with salt and set aside for 30 minutes. Rinse aubergines and scoop out the flesh, leaving a border to form a firm shell. Blanch the aubergine shells in boiling water for 3 minutes, then drain. Chop the flesh.

Heat the oil in a frying pan and fry the onion and garlic until softened. Stir in the pepper, mushrooms and aubergine flesh and fry for 5 minutes. Add the tomatoes, tomato purée, basil and sugar. Season well. Place the hollowed out aubergine shells in a lightly greased, shallow ovenproof dish and pile the tomato mixture into the shells. Mix together the breadcrumbs, oregano, walnuts and cheese, if using. Sprinkle over the aubergines. Bake in an oven preheated to 190°C/375°F/Gas Mark 5, for 20 minutes. Serve with a salad garnish.

Time: Preparation takes about 20 minutes, plus standing. Cooking takes about 40 minutes.

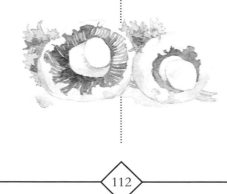

Sesame Stir-Fry

This recipe can be prepared in advance and cooked quickly for a convenient Oriental meal.

SERVES 4

2 tbsps vegetable oil

½ tsp grated fresh root ginger

15g/½oz sesame seeds

60g/2oz mange tout peas

1 stick celery, sliced

2 baby corn cobs, cut in half lengthways

60g/2oz water chestnuts, thinly sliced

30g/1oz mushrooms, thinly sliced

2 spring onions, sliced diagonally

½ red pepper, sliced

120g/4oz Chinese leaves, washed and shredded

120g/4oz bean sprouts

1 tbsp cornflour

2 tbsps soy sauce

1 tbsp sherry

½ tsp sesame oil

60ml/4 tbsps water

Heat the oil in a wok or large frying pan and fry the ginger and sesame seeds for 1 minute. Add the mange tout peas, celery, baby corn, water chestnuts, mushrooms, spring onions and pepper. Stir-fry for 5 minutes or until the vegetables are beginning to soften slightly. Add the Chinese leaves and bean sprouts and toss over the heat for 1-2 minutes.

Combine the remaining ingredients in a small bowl, then add to the pan. Continue cooking until sauce thickens slightly and serve immediately.

Time: Preparation takes about 15 minutes, cooking takes about 10 minutes.

Variation: Use any combination of vegetables according to what you have at hand.

Kidney Bean Curry

Kidney beans are wonderfully enhanced by the flavour of spices in this delicious curry.

SERVES 4

2 tbsps vegetable oil

1 large onion, sliced

2 cloves garlic, crushed

2 green chillies, seeded and chopped

2 tsps grated fresh root ginger

1 tsp chilli powder

1 tsp ground coriander

1 tsp ground cumin

1 tsp garam masala

1 cinnamon stick

400g/14oz can chopped tomatoes

1 bay leaf

450g/1lb canned red kidney beans, drained weight

Salt and freshly ground black pepper

Chopped fresh coriander, to garnish

Heat the oil in a large saucepan and fry the onion, garlic and fresh chillies for 5 minutes. Stir in the spices and cook for 1 minute. Add the tomatoes, bay leaf and kidney beans. Season to taste. Cover and simmer gently for 30 minutes or until the flavours are well blended. Remove the cinnamon stick and bay leaf. Garnish with chopped coriander.

Time: Preparation takes about 20 minutes, cooking takes about 35 minutes.

Serving Idea: Serve with a cucumber raita or hot lime pickle. Naan bread or chapattis are also excellent accompaniments.

Preparation: Great care must be taken when preparing fresh chillies. Wear rubber gloves to prevent the juice being left on the fingers and getting into your eyes or mouth. If this should happen, rinse with plenty of cold water.

Festive Roast

Never again will Christmas dinner be a problem with this festive roast.

SERVES 8

2 tbsps sunflower oil
2 medium onions, finely chopped
2 cloves garlic, crushed
450g/1lb finely ground cashew nuts
225g/8oz wholemeal breadcrumbs
2 beaten eggs or 4 tbsps soya flour mixed with a little water
1 heaped tsp mixed herbs
2 tsps Marmite or yeast extract
280ml/½ pint boiling water
Salt and pepper

Heat the oil and fry the onion and garlic until soft. Place the onions and garlic into a large bowl. Add all the other ingredients and mix well. Butter or line a 2lb loaf tin and spoon in the mixture. Cover with a double thickness of foil and cook in an oven preheated to 180°C/350°F/Gas Mark 4, for about 1 hour 20 minutes until firm. Allow to cool for about 10 minutes in the tin before turning out.

Time: Preparation takes about 15 minutes, cooking takes about 1 hour 20 minutes.

Freezing: An excellent dish to freeze cooked or uncooked, although a slightly better result is obtained if frozen uncooked and thawed overnight in the refrigerator.

Serving Idea: Serve with a wine sauce or gravy and decorate with sprigs of holly.

Carrot and Cashew Nut Roast

A delicious roast to serve hot, although the full flavour of the caraway seeds and lemon is more prominent when the roast is served cold.

SERVES 6

1 medium-sized onion, chopped
1-2 cloves garlic, crushed
1 tbsp olive or sunflower oil
450g/1lb carrots, cooked and mashed
225g/8oz cashew nuts, ground
120g/4oz wholewheat breadcrumbs
1 tbsp light tahini
1½ tsps caraway seeds
1 tsp yeast extract
Juice of ½ a lemon
65ml/2½fl oz stock from the carrots, or water
Salt and freshly ground black pepper

Fry the onion and garlic in the oil until soft. Mix together with all the other ingredients and season to taste. Place the mixture in a greased 900g/2lb loaf tin. Cover with foil and bake in an oven preheated to 180°C/350°F/Gas Mark 4, for 1 hour.

Remove the foil and bake for a further 10 minutes. Leave to stand in the baking tin for at least 10 minutes before turning out.

Time: Preparation takes 20 minutes, cooking takes 1 hour 10 minutes.

Serving Idea: Serve hot with roast potatoes and a green vegetable, or cold with a mixed green salad.

Side Dishes

Side dishes can transform a rather ordinary main dish into a memorable meal. If for convenience you have prepared a simple vegetable burger, grill or omelette, then go to town with an unusual accompaniment. Because vegetarians tend to eat rather more vegetables than meat eaters by incorporating them more often into main courses, there's more reason than ever to take the trouble to serve accompanying vegetables in a rather more elaborate way.

It's also nice to give seasonal produce a distinctive touch when it is at its most plentiful such as in Brussels Sprouts with Hazelnuts (p. 120) or Spinach with Blue Cheese and Walnuts (p. 118).

Other accompaniments are perfect at any time of the year – don't forget rice as a simple, nutritious side dish. Being a protein-containing grain, rice is helpful in boosting the protein content of vegetarian food, and is especially beneficial when served with a nut- or bean-based dish.

Good old potatoes shouldn't be overlooked either; if the oven is being used for a slow cooking dish, pop a baked potato in to cook too. Summer's fresh new potatoes can be served with just about any dish, garnished with a little mint, chives or parsley from the herb garden. Other root vegetables work well too, often in association with each other. Instead of just plain mashed potatoes, try adding

parsnip or swede, or combining colourful carrot and swede in one dramatic purée.

Don't forget to use the microwave for cooking vegetables. A microwave is excellent for cooking small quantities of fresh vegetables in just the minimum of water. It's also ideal for cooking frozen vegetables straight from the freezer. Always remember to time food carefully as it is all too easy to overcook vegetables in the microwave, and to lose that lovely, barely soft texture.

Whether cooking vegetables by microwave or by conventional means, always try to remember the golden rules of vegetable (and fruit) preparation. To ensure maximum retention of vitamin C prepare immediately before cooking, in the minimum of water to limit the loss of the water-soluble vitamins B and C. Cook until just tender – overcooking destroys the texture, flavour and vitamin C content, as does keeping vegetables warm in a heated dish until required. Try to save cooking water from vegetables and use it in sauces, soups and gravies.

Finally, don't forget how easy it is to stir-fry vegetables to liven up a main course. Finely sliced root vegetables, shredded green leaves, sliced peppers, mushrooms or courgettes and broccoli all make colourful stir-fries. Cook quickly in a wok or large frying pan in a little oil, with a hint of garlic, ginger or soy sauce to give an Oriental touch to your vegetables.

Spinach with Blue Cheese — & Walnuts —

This hot salad is an ideal accompaniment to a rich meal.

SERVES 4

900g/2lbs spinach, washed
30g/1oz butter or margarine
Pinch of grated nutmeg
Salt and freshly ground black pepper
120g/4oz walnuts, roughly chopped
120g/4oz vegetarian blue cheese, crumbled

Remove any tough leaves from the spinach and place the leaves in a saucepan with just the water left clinging to them after washing. Cook over a low heat for 5-10 minutes until the spinach wilts. Put the spinach onto a plate and press a second plate firmly on top to remove the excess water.

Melt the butter or margarine in the pan and stir in the spinach along with the nutmeg and seasoning. Stir well to coat evenly. Quickly stir in the walnuts and cheese, tossing the ingredients together lightly. Serve quickly before the cheese melts too much.

Time: Preparation takes about 15 minutes, cooking takes about 10 minutes.
Serving Idea: Serve with nut roasts, vegetable cutlets or pâtés.
Variation: Use diced tofu instead of cheese in this recipe for a vegan alternative.

Braised Fennel

The aromatic, aniseed flavour of fennel makes it an ideal accompaniment to rich casseroles and vegetable bakes.

SERVES 4

2 large bulbs of fennel
2 tsps chopped fresh lovage
120ml/4fl oz vegetable stock
2 tbsps sherry
½ tsp celery seeds or celery seasoning

With a sharp knife, cut away the thick root end of the fennel bulbs. Trim away the upper stalks and reserve a little of the green top for a garnish. Thickly slice the fennel, separating the strips from each other as you cut. Place the fennel, lovage, stock and sherry in a saucepan and bring to the boil. Reduce the heat and simmer gently for about 15 minutes or until the fennel is tender. Drain and transfer to a warm serving dish. Sprinkle with celery seeds or seasoning and garnish with fennel tops.
Time: Preparation takes about 10 minutes, cooking takes about 15 minutes.

Cook's Tip: If lovage is unavailable, use some of the leafy fennel tops, chopped, instead.
Variation: Add 1 peeled, cored and thinly sliced cooking apple to the fennel for a delicious variation.

Wild Rice Pilau

Although expensive, a little wild rice goes a long way when mixed with long-grain rice, adding a special flavour and texture to the dish.

SERVES 4

175g/6oz long-grain rice

60g/2oz wild rice

2 tbsps vegetable oil

1 piece cassia bark or ½ stick cinnamon

4 black or green cardamom pods, lightly crushed

8 cloves

4 black peppercorns

1 piece star anise

570ml/1 pint vegetable stock

60ml/4 tbsps dry white wine

60g/2oz flaked almonds

60g/2oz raisins

Place the rices in two separate sieves and rinse thoroughly under running water, draining each well. Heat half the oil in a saucepan and fry all the spices for 1 minute. Stir in the wild rice and cook for 1 minute, stirring constantly. Add the stock and wine and bring to the boil. Stir, cover and simmer for 30 minutes.

Just before the 30 minutes is up, heat the remaining oil in a frying pan, add the long-grain rice and cook, stirring, for 1 minute. Add some of the hot liquid from the wild rice to the frying pan and stir in. Pour the long-grain rice and liquid into the wild rice and stir well. Cover the pan and simmer for a further 20-30 minutes, or until the rice is tender and most of the liquid has been absorbed. If the rice is still hard when most of the liquid has been absorbed, add a little water. Stir the remaining ingredients into the pan and allow to stand covered for 5 minutes, until the liquid is completely absorbed. Fluff up the rice with a fork before serving.

Time: Preparation takes about 5 minutes, cooking takes about 1 hour.

Serving Idea: Serve with vegetarian curries, casseroles or salads.

Variation: Add some cooked chopped mixed vegetables instead of the nuts and raisins.

Carrot & Parsnip Medley

The perfect accompaniment to the recipe for Festive Roast
(see page 115)

SERVES 8

90g/3oz butter or margarine
8 medium carrots, peeled and sliced
4 parsnips, peeled and cut into rings
1 tsp ground ginger
½ tsp grated nutmeg
Salt and freshly ground black pepper
Juice of 1 lemon
2 tsps caster sugar
Chopped fresh parsley

Melt the butter or margarine in a large pan and add the carrots and parsnips. Sauté very gently for 2-3 minutes then add the ginger, nutmeg, seasoning, lemon juice and enough water to cover the vegetables. Cover and simmer for 15-20 minutes until the vegetables are soft and the liquid has evaporated.

Add the sugar and increase the heat, tossing the vegetables until they are glossy. Transfer to a heated serving dish and sprinkle with the chopped parsley.

Time: Preparation takes 10 minutes, cooking takes 20-25 minutes.
Variation: Any chopped fresh herbs may be used for garnishing – coriander is a good alternative.
Cook's Tip: Lemons yield more juice if you first roll them backwards and forwards on a kitchen work surface with your hands using medium pressure.

Brussels Sprouts with — Hazelnuts —

This is a delicious variation on Brussels sprouts with chestnuts and will soon become a firm favourite.

SERVES 4

450g/1lb Brussel sprouts, trimmed
30g/1oz butter or margarine
60g/2oz hazelnuts
Salt and freshly ground black pepper

Cut a cross in the stalks of any large sprouts and cook in lightly salted boiling water for 10-15 minutes or until tender. Just before the sprouts are cooked, melt the butter or margarine in a frying pan and fry the hazelnuts, stirring frequently, until browned.

When the sprouts are cooked, drain well and return to the pan. Add the hazelnuts and toss well. Transfer to a serving dish and serve with a good sprinkling of black pepper.

Time: Preparation takes about 10 minutes, cooking takes about 15 minutes.
Serving Idea: Serve with grills and nut roasts.
Variation: Use almonds or peanuts instead of hazelnuts in this recipe.

Pommes Noisettes

These delicious cheesy potato balls will complement any meal, whether a sophisticated dinner party or a homely family meal.

SERVES 4-6

450g/1lb potatoes, peeled and cut into chunks
30g/1oz butter or margarine
Salt and freshly ground black pepper
60g/2oz vegetarian Gruyère or Edam-type cheese, finely grated
60g/2oz ground hazelnuts
Oil for shallow-frying
Fresh parsley or watercress sprigs, to garnish

Cook the potatoes until tender; mash well. Add the butter or margarine, seasoning and cheese, and fork through until well combined. Refrigerate until completely cold. Shape spoonfuls of the mashed potatoes into 2.5cm/1-inch balls.

Spread the nuts on a plate and roll the potato balls in the nuts, making sure they are well coated. Heat the oil in a frying pan and fry the potato until golden, turning frequently. Serve garnished with parsley or watercress.

Time: Preparation takes about 15 minutes, plus chilling. Cooking takes about 30 minutes.

Serving Idea: Serve with grills, salads or roasts.

Preparation: The noisettes can be prepared up to 24 hours in advance.

Variation: Use peanuts instead of hazelnuts in this recipe.

Perfect Potatoes

Potatoes become extra special when teamed up with the flavour of onion.

SERVES 5

900g/2lbs potatoes
1 large onion
Salt and freshly ground black pepper
280ml/½pint milk
45g/1½oz butter or margarine

Peel and finely slice the potatoes and onion. Layer the potato slices and onion in a shallow ovenproof dish, sprinkling each layer with some salt and pepper. Pour over the milk and dot with the butter or margarine. Bake uncovered in an oven preheated to 180°C/350°F/Gas Mark 4, for 1-1½ hours or until the potatoes are soft, and golden brown on top.

Time: Preparation takes 15 minutes, cooking takes 1-1½ hours.

Serving Idea: Serve with grilled mushrooms and tomatoes for a supper dish or serve with nut roasts or pies.

Freezing: Cool quickly, cover with foil and place in a freezer bag. Defrost at room temperature for 4-6 hours and reheat at 190°C/375°F/Gas Mark 5 for about 30 minutes.

Variation: Place a layer of finely sliced cooking apples in the bottom of the dish.

Sri Lankan Rice

Serve this rice hot as an accompaniment to vegetable curries or dhal.

SERVES 12

3 tbsps sunflower oil
1 medium onion, finely chopped
2 cloves garlic, crushed
1 heaped tsp ground cumin
1 heaped tsp ground coriander
1 heaped tsp paprika
2 tsps turmeric
¼ tsp chilli or cayenne pepper
150g/5oz Basmati rice, washed and drained
340ml/12fl oz milk
1 tsp salt
Freshly ground black pepper to taste
225g/8oz mange tout, topped, tailed and cut in half
120g/4oz mushrooms, washed and sliced
150g/5oz can sweetcorn, drained
60g/2oz sultanas, washed and soaked

Heat the oil in a large non-stick pan. Gently fry the onion and garlic for 4-5 minutes. Add the cumin, coriander, paprika, turmeric and chilli, and fry for a further 3-4 minutes – do not allow the mixture to burn. Add the washed rice, mix well with the onions and spices and cook for about 2 minutes. Add the milk, salt and pepper, stir gently, bring to the boil, cover and simmer until all the liquid is absorbed and the rice is cooked – approximately 15-20 minutes.

Whilst the rice is cooking, steam the mange tout, mushrooms, sweetcorn and sultanas and fold into the rice. Cool and turn out onto a serving dish.

Time: Preparation takes 15 minutes, cooking takes 25-30 minutes.

Serving Idea: Sprinkle with 2 tbsps of freshly chopped coriander or parsley.

Variation: Other lightly steamed vegetables may be used according to season and personal taste – broccoli florets, diced carrots, peas and sliced green peppers.

Leeks Provençale

This classic method of serving vegetables is exceptionally well suited to leeks as the flavours combine so well.

SERVES 4

6 leeks, washed and trimmed
1 tbsp olive oil
2 cloves garlic, crushed
4 tomatoes, skinned, seeded and chopped
1 tsp dried thyme
2 tbsps chopped fresh parsley
60ml/4 tbsps dry white wine
Salt and freshly ground black pepper
Sprigs of fresh parsley, to garnish

Cut the leeks into 5cm/2-inch pieces. Cook the leeks for 10-15 minutes in lightly salted boiling water, until tender. Heat the oil in a small saucepan and fry the garlic until softened but not coloured. Stir in the tomatoes, herbs and wine and simmer gently for 10 minutes or until the tomatoes are softened. Season to taste. When the leeks are cooked, drain well and place in a serving dish. Spoon the tomato mixture into the dish and turn the leeks in the sauce to coat. Serve garnished with a sprig of parsley.
Time: Preparation takes about 10 minutes, cooking takes about 25 minutes.
Serving Idea: Serve with any vegetarian meal.

Sweet & Sour Cabbage —with Apple—

This tasty side dish adds a splash of colour as well as a lively flavour to any meal.

SERVES 4

1.4kg/3lbs red cabbage
1 onion, chopped
1 cooking apple, peeled, cored and chopped
60g/2oz light muscovado sugar
¼ tsp ground mixed spice
Salt and freshly ground black pepper
140ml/½ pint vegetable stock
2 tbsps red wine vinegar
1 tbsp walnut oil
1 dessert apple, cored and chopped
2 tsps chopped fresh parsley

Quarter, core and shred the cabbage and layer in a large saucepan with the onion and cooking apple. Sprinkle with the sugar and mixed spice. Season with salt and pepper. Add the stock and vinegar and stir to mix the ingredients well. Cover and cook gently for 45 minutes, stirring occasionally.

Just before the end of the cooking time, heat the oil in a frying pan and sauté the dessert apple for 2-3 minutes until just soft. Remove from the heat and stir in the parsley. Transfer the cabbage to a serving dish and garnish with the apple and parsley.
Time: Preparation takes about 20 minutes, cooking takes about 45 minutes.

Broccoli and Cauliflower — Mould —

Although this dish takes a little while to prepare, it makes a spectacular addition to the dinner table.

SERVES 4-6

1 small cauliflower
225g/8oz broccoli
3 tbsps walnut oil
1 tbsp white wine vinegar
1 tsp mustard powder
½ clove garlic, crushed
Salt and freshly ground black pepper
1 tbsp olive oil
1 green chilli, seeded and finely chopped
5 tomatoes, skinned, seeded and chopped
1 green pepper, finely chopped
1 tsp ground cumin
4 spring onions, finely chopped
Tomato quarters, to garnish

Divide the cauliflower into florets and discard the thick stalks. Trim the broccoli to within 5cm/2 inches of the florets. Bring a saucepan of water to the boil, add the cauliflower and cook for 5 minutes. Add the broccoli, cook a further 10 minutes, and then drain well.

Combine the walnut oil, vinegar, mustard, garlic and salt and pepper in a small bowl and whisk with a fork. Pour the dressing over the warm vegetables and toss to coat well, taking care not to break them up. Carefully arrange the cauliflower and broccoli in a deep-sided 570ml/1-pint bowl, alternating the 2 vegetables and pressing them together lightly to push them firmly into the bowl shape. Cover with a plate and weigh down slightly. Leave to cool, before refrigerating it ready for serving.

Heat the olive oil in a small pan and fry the chilli for 2-3 minutes, add the tomatoes, pepper, cumin and spring onions. Cook for 5 minutes. Season with salt and pepper, allow to cool, then refrigerate well before serving. To serve, carefully turn out the cauliflower mould onto a serving plate and spoon the tomato salsa around the base. Garnish with tomato quarters.

Time: Preparation takes about 20 minutes, plus chilling. Cooking takes about 20 minutes.

Courgette Rolls

These artistic little vegetable rolls are an impressive way of serving an accompaniment to a sophisticated meal.

SERVES 4

2 carrots, peeled and cut into thin sticks
2 green peppers, cut into strips
4 spring onions, trimmed
Salt and freshly ground black pepper
1 tsp chopped fresh basil or thyme
2 large courgettes
Juice of 1 lemon
Bunch of fresh chives
30g/1oz butter or margarine
2 tbsps vegetable oil

Cook the carrots and green peppers for 5 minutes in boiling water until just softened. Drain well and place in a mixing bowl. Shred the spring onions lengthways and add to the carrots and pepper. Season the vegetables, add the chopped herbs and toss together thoroughly. Trim the courgettes and carefully cut lengthways into very thin slices. Sprinkle with the lemon juice. Lay out the courgette strips on the work surface and arrange bundles of the vegetables in piles across them. Carefully roll up the courgette strips around the vegetables. Secure them by tying at each end with chives.

Melt the butter or margarine with the oil in a frying pan and sauté the vegetable bundles for 10 minutes, turning frequently until the courgettes are cooked and the vegetables are hot.
Time: Preparation takes 20 minutes, cooking takes 20 minutes.

Tasty Tomato Sauce

Serve this adaptable sauce over stuffed aubergines, marrow or peppers.

SERVES 4

30g/1oz pine nuts
Pinch of salt
1 tsp sunflower oil
1 onion, chopped
Pinch of chilli powder
3 cloves
400g/14oz can tomatoes

Place the pine nuts in a frying pan and dry roast. Remove when they are lightly browned and sprinkle with the salt. Fry the onion in the sunflower oil until soft. Add the chilli powder and cloves. Fry for 1 minute. Add the tomatoes, bring to the boil and simmer for 10 minutes. Cool slightly and remove the cloves. Blend the mixture in a liquidiser and return to pan. Add the pine nuts and reheat gently.
Time: Preparation takes 10 minutes, cooking takes 15 minutes.
Watchpoint: Dry roast the pine nuts over a low heat, stirring continuously, otherwise they will burn.

Desserts

When it comes to dessert, most people can be tempted by a little serving of something sweet, so choose your final course with care to balance with the rest of the meal. From a nutritional point of view, if a meal has been quite light on protein with the emphasis on vegetables rather than dairy produce or beans or nuts, now's the time to serve a dairy-based dessert – a cheescake perhaps, or a heavier, traditional style pie or crumble, or even a deliciously different fruit pizza (see Hot Apple Pizza p.131).

Fruit, full of vitamins and fibre, forms a nutritious basis for many popular desserts, whether hot, cold or frozen. While it's easy to stock the freezer with commercial ice creams and sorbets, there's nothing quite like a home-made ice to impress your guests. Choose either a rich cream or custard based ice or a refreshing, tangy fruit sorbet, such as Strawberry Sorbet (p.138). Fruit fools, light and easy on the stomach, make a similarly simple end to a meal, perhaps served with a home-made biscuit or piece of shortbread. And why not follow the season's fruits by serving a Cranberry Fool (p.137) at Christmas?

Giving old family favourites a new twist always works well – Cranberry and Apple Crumble (p.132) for example or Baked Raspberry Apples (p.129). Baked apples are also delicious stuffed with marzipan, a tasty way of boosting the protein level of a pudding, and can be 'baked' in the microwave to save time, but watch carefully to avoid overcooking. Cored pears are also suitable for baking filled with a sweet mixture of fresh or dried fruit – also delicious topped with home-made custard. Vegans avoiding dairy produce could try a topping of tofu blended with a little sugar and a touch of vanilla or almond, or even a hint of spice such as nutmeg or cinnamon.

One dessert which always proves a winner without piling on the calories is fresh fruit salad. Here the possibilities for combining different fruits are almost endless. Rather than preparing a sugar-based syrup, simply pour over a little fruit juice – orange, freshly pressed apple, grape or a fruit cocktail blend, with just a hint of Cointreau perhaps. A large bowl full of a myriad different fruits looks stunning, but also consider restricting choice and sticking instead to a colour theme. A bowl full of luscious red fruits looks superb, as does a subtle mix of pale peaches and green from grapes, kiwi fruit, peaches, galia, or cantaloupe melon and oranges. Alternatively for a different effect again, rather than tossing all together, try arranging different fruits in different layers. However it is served, choose your dessert to end any meal on a high note.

Windward Fruit Basket

An impressive dessert which is surprisingly easy to prepare.

SERVES 4-6

1 large ripe melon
2 apples
Juice of 1 lime
2 mangoes
2 kiwi fruit
450g/1lb strawberries, hulled
225g/¹⁄₂lb rasperries
3 tbsps honey
2 tbsps dark rum
60g/2oz butter

Cut the top off the melon and scoop out the seeds. Using a melon baller, scoop out balls of melon and place in a large bowl. Remove the core from the apples, dice and toss in the lime juice. Peel and chop the mangoes. Peel and slice the kiwi fruit. Combine the prepared fruits with the whole strawberries and raspberries. Heat the honey, rum and butter gently until the butter has melted. Cool, and pour over the fruits. Toss gently and fill the melon shell with the fruit mixture. Place on a serving dish and serve immediately.

Time: Preparation takes 20 minutes, cooking takes 2 minutes.

Serving Idea: For a special occasion, make holes around the top of the melon with a skewer and decorate with fresh flowers.

Variation: Use any fresh fruits in season, pears, peaches etc.

Strawberry & Banana Frost

This speedy dessert can be started ahead of time and completed just before serving.

SERVES 4-6

450g/1lb strawberries
1 large banana
175ml/6fl oz fromage frais
Few drops of vanilla essence
1 tsp clear honey

Wash and hull the strawberries and put half of them in the refrigerator. Peel the banana and cut into pieces. Cut the remaining strawberries in halves, quarters if they are large, and freeze with the banana until solid. Just before serving, remove the strawberries and banana from the freezer. Place the frozen strawberries and banana with the fromage frais, vanilla essence and honey in a food processor or liquidiser and process until smooth. You will need to push the mixture down two or three times with a spatula or wooden spoon. Divide the mixture between 4 or 6 individual serving dishes and place the remaining strawberries around the 'frost' mixture. Serve at once.

Time: Preparation takes 10 minutes, freezing takes at least 1 hour.

Variation: Pineapple, raspberries or apple can be substituted for the above.

Baked Raspberry Apples

A lovely combination which is perfectly complemented
by cream or yogurt.

SERVES 6

2 tbsps concentrated apple juice
60ml/4 tbsps water
2 tbsps honey
1 tsp mixed spice
3 very large dessert apples
225g/8oz raspberries

Put the concentrated apple juice, water, honey and mixed spice into a large bowl and mix together well. Wash the apples and, with a sharp knife, make deep zig zag cuts around each apple. Take one half of the apple in each hand and twist gently until the two halves come apart. Remove the core and immerse each apple in the apple juice mixture. Place the apples in an ovenproof dish and bake in an oven preheated to 200°C/400°F/Gas Mark 6, for 20-25 minutes until just soft.

Remove from the oven and top with the raspberries. Pour the remaining apple juice mixture over the raspberries and return to the oven at the reduced temprature of 150°C/300°F/Gas Mark 2 for 10 minutes. Serve at once.
Time: Preparation takes 10 minutes, cooking takes 30-35 minutes.
Serving Idea: Serve topped with a spoonful of Greek yogurt or whipped cream.
Cook's Tip: Frozen raspberries may be used but make sure they are defrosted first.

Raspberry Meringues

Light, pale pink meringues form the basis of this
delightful summer dessert.

SERVES 4

2 egg whites
120g/4oz caster sugar
Few drops raspberry flavouring
Few drops of red food colouring (optional)
225g/8oz raspberries (optional)
60ml/4 tbsps raspberry liqueur or sherry
140ml/¼ pint double cream, whipped
Cocoa powder, for decoration

Line two baking sheets with non-stick baking parchment. Whisk the egg whites until stiff, then gradually whisk in the two-thirds of the caster sugar. Carefully fold in the remaining sugar, flavouring and a food colouring, if using. Spoon into a piping bag fitted with a plain nozzle and pipe eight heart shapes or rounds.

Place in an oven preheated to 150°C/300°F/Gas Mark 2 for 1½ hours to dry out. Remove from the oven and allow to cool completely. Meanwhile, place the raspberries and liqueur or sherry in a bowl and allow to marinate until required. Whip the cream and use, together with a few of the soaked raspberries, to sandwich the meringues into pairs. Sprinkle the tops with a little cocoa powder and serve any remaining raspberries separately.
Time: Preparation takes about 20 minutes, cooking takes about 1½ hours.
Serving Idea: Serve with extra fruit salad if a more substantial dessert is required.

Peachy Cheesecake

This fairly rich cheesecake has a lovely smooth texture.

SERVES 6

Base

12 digestive biscuits, crushed into fine crumbs

40g/1½ oz melted butter or margarine

Topping

400g/14oz curd cheese

430ml/15fl oz soured cream or Greek yogurt

2 tbsps clear honey

1½ tsps vanilla essence or lemon juice

2 eggs, beaten

1½ tbsps wholewheat self-raising flour

Sliced peaches to decorate

Combine the biscuit crumbs, melted butter and spices and press the mixture in the bottom of a greased 23cm/9-inch flan tin or dish. Combine the curd cheese and 200ml/7 fl oz of the soured cream or yogurt, 1 tbsp honey, ¾ tsp vanilla essence, the eggs and all the flour. Pour the mixture onto the biscuit base and bake in an oven preheated to 150°C/300°F/Gas Mark 2 for about 20 minutes or until just set. Remove from the oven and increase the temperature to 230°C/450°F/Gas Mark 8.

Combine the remaining cream or yogurt with the rest of the honey and vanilla essence and spread over the top of the cake. Smooth over with a knife or spatula. Return to the oven and bake for 5 minutes. Allow to cool before decorating with sliced peaches. Chill thoroughly before serving.

Time: Preparation takes 25 minutes, cooking takes 25 minutes.

Variation: For special occasions decorate with seasonal fruit such as strawberries or raspberries and chocolate or carob curls.

Cook's Tip: Canned fruit may be used if fresh is not available.

Fruit Salad Cups

These attractive cups of warm fresh fruit make a delightful and unusual ending to a meal.

SERVES 4

2 large oranges
1 small dessert apple
1 slice of fresh pineapple
1 banana
A little orange juice
30g/1oz caster sugar
1 tsp rum
15g/1½oz pistachio nuts, skin removed and chopped
Orange zest, to decorate (optional)

Cut the oranges in half and, using a grapefruit knife, remove the flesh and membranes, leaving just the white pith and zest to form a shell. Set aside. Reserve as much juice as possible and chop the flesh, discarding tough membranes. Cut the apple into quarters, remove the core but do not peel. Cut each quarter into bite-size pieces. Remove the skin and any brown 'eyes' from the pineapple and cut the flesh into bite-sized wedges. Peel and slice the banana.

Make the reserved juice up to 140ml/¼ pint with extra orange juice, if necessary. Heat the juice and sugar and stir until dissolved. Stir in the rum. Mix the prepared fruit into the juice. Just before serving, heat gently to warm the fruit but not cook it. Pile into the orange shells and sprinkle with the chopped pistachio nuts. Decorate with orange zest, if wished, and serve immediately.
Time: Preparation takes 15 minutes, cooking takes 5 minutes.

Hot Apple Pizza

A delicious dessert – perfect with yogurt or cream.

SERVES 4-6

15g/½oz fresh yeast
60ml/2fl oz warm water
90g/3oz strong wholemeal flour
60g/2oz strong white flour
½ tsp ground cinnamon
15g/½oz butter or margarine
1/2 tbsp concentrated apple juice

Topping
2 red skinned dessert apples
30g/1oz raisins
30g/1oz hazelnuts
1 tbsp concentrated apple juice
15g/½oz butter or margarine

Cream the yeast with the water, add 1 teaspoon of flour and leave in a warm place for 10-15 minutes until frothy. Mix together the flours and cinnamon. Rub in the butter. Add the yeast mixture and concentrated apple juice to the flour. Mix to a stiff dough, adding more warm water if necessary. Knead well. Roll the dough into a circle, about 23cm/8-9 inches. Cover with cling film and leave to rise for 10-15 minutes.

Slice the apples evenly and arrange over the base. Sprinkle the raisins, hazelnuts and concentrated apple juice over the apples and dot with the butter or margarine. Bake in the middle shelf of an oven preheated to 200°C/400°F/Gas Mark 6, for 15-20 minutes.
Time: Preparation takes, including rising, 45 minutes. Cooking takes 15-20 minutes.

Cranberry and Apple Crumble

Serve hot with natural yogurt or cold with ice cream.

SERVES 4

680g/1½lbs Bramley or other cooking apples

60g/2oz caster sugar

175g/6oz fresh cranberries

Crumble

90g/3oz butter or margarine

60g/2oz sunflower seeds

90g/3oz demerara sugar

150g/5oz wholewheat flour

60g/2oz jumbo oats

60g/2oz porridge oats

Peel, core and dice the apples. Place in a saucepan with the sugar and about 2 tbsps water. Cook gently until just beginning to soften. Add the cranberries and cook for a further minute. Remove from the heat.

Melt the butter or margarine in a small saucepan, add the sunflower seeds and fry very gently for a few minutes. Mix together the other ingredients in a large bowl, rubbing in the sugar with the fingers if lumpy. Pour the butter and sunflower seeds into this mixture and combine to form a loose crumble. Place the fruit in a large, shallow ovenproof dish and sprinkle the crumble topping over. Bake in an oven preheated to 180°C/350°F/Gas Mark 4, for about 40 minutes or until the top is golden and crisp.

Time: Preparation takes about 20 minutes, cooking takes 50 minutes.

Low-Fat Brown Bread Ice Cream

This ice cream is ideal for slimmers.

SERVES 4

35g/1½oz brown breadcrumbs

35g/1½oz brown sugar

3 eggs, separated

280ml/½ pint Greek yogurt

2 tsps honey (optional)

Place the breadcrumbs on a baking tray and cover with the sugar. Place in an oven preheated to 190°C/375°F/Gas Mark 5 for 20 minutes or until they begin to brown and caramelise. Stir once or twice so they brown evenly. Leave aside. Beat the egg whites until stiff.

In a separate bowl, mix the egg yolks into the yogurt and then fold in the egg whites. Add the honey if wished and fold in evenly. Add the cold breadcrumbs and mix well. Place in the freezer and when setting point is reached stir the sides to prevent ice crystals forming. Return to the freezer and leave until set.

Time: Preparation takes 20 minutes, cooking and freezing takes 20 minutes plus 4-5 hours or overnight.

Cook's Tip: Remove from the freezer and place in the refrigerator about ¾ of an hour before serving.

Variation: Maple syrup may be used in place of honey.

St Clement's Sorbet

St. Clement's is possibly the most popular type of sorbet, and it is really quite simple to make your own.

SERVES 6

280ml/¹/₂ pint water
225g/8oz granulated sugar
4 lemons
1 tbsp agar-agar
570ml/1 pint freshly squeezed orange juice
2 egg whites
Grated orange zest and mint leaves, to decorate

Place the water and sugar in a saucepan, heat gently until the sugar dissolves, bring to the boil and boil for 5 minutes. Remove from the heat and allow to cool completely. Grate the rind from the lemons with a zester and squeeze the juice. Put a little of the lemon juice in a small bowl and sprinkle over the agar-agar. Dissolve over hot water.

Combine the cooled sugar syrup, lemon rind, juice, dissolved agar-agar and orange juice; pour into a shallow freezer-proof container and freeze until slushy. Remove from the freezer and beat well to break up the ice crystals. Whisk the egg whites until they stand in soft peaks and beat into the sorbet mixture. Cover and freeze until required. Serve scooped into serving glasses and decorated with orange zest and mint leaves.

Time: Preparation takes about 30 minutes, plus freezing.
Serving Idea: Spoon the sorbet into hollowed out lemon or orange halves.

Fruit Fantasia

A pretty dessert which is simple to prepare and very refreshing.

SERVES 8

1 melon
4 large grapefruit
120g/4oz black grapes
120g/4oz green dessert apples
2 red dessert apples
140ml/¹/₄ pint single cream
Mint leaves to decorate

Cut the melon into quarters. Remove the flesh, cut into 2.5cm/1-inch pieces and place in a large bowl. Make zig-zag cuts around each grapefruit, halve, remove the flesh and add to the melon, reserving the grapefruit shells. Halve and seed the grapes. Wash the apples and slice finely, leaving the skin on. Add to the grapefruit, grapes and melon. Chill for at least 1 hour. Mix the single cream carefully into the fruit and pile into the grapefruit shells. Decorate with the mint before serving.

Time: Preparation takes about 10 minutes, chilling takes at least 1 hour.
Serving Idea: Serve in individual dishes containing crushed ice and decorated with mint leaves.
Variation: If time is short use seedless grapes and leave whole.

Crêpes Suzette

Most of the preparation for this spectacular dinner party dish can be done well in advance.

SERVES 4

120g/4oz plain flour
¼ tsp ground nutmeg
2 eggs
2 tsps vegetable oil
280ml/½ pint milk
Oil for frying
60g/2oz butter or margarine
Grated rind of 1 orange
60g/2oz caster sugar
225ml/8fl oz fresh orange juice
2 tbsps orange-flavoured liqueur
2 tbsps brandy
Orange slices, to decorate

Sift the flour and nutmeg into a mixing bowl and make a well in the centre. Drop the eggs, oil and a little of the milk into the well. Beat well using a wooden spoon, slowly incorporating the flour until you have a smooth paste. Gradually beat in the remaining milk, then allow to stand for 20 minutes. Heat a little oil in a 20.5cm/8-inch heavy-based frying pan. Pour off the excess. Spoon about 3 tbsps of the batter into the pan and tilt the pan so that the batter coats the base. Cook for about 1 minute until the underside is golden, then flip or turn over and cook the other side.

Slide the pancake out of the pan and set aside. Repeat until all the batter has been used, stacking the pancakes on top of each other. Cover to prevent them drying out.

Melt the butter or margarine in a frying pan and stir in the orange rind, sugar and juice. Cook, stirring, until the sugar dissolves. Add the orange liqueur and allow to boil gently for a few minutes until the liquid has reduced slightly.

Fold the pancakes into triangles and add to the pan. Cook gently to warm the pancakes through. Heat the brandy in a small pan. Set alight and pour over the pancakes. Serve when the flames have died down. Decorate with orange slices.

Time: Preparation takes about 35 minutes, plus standing. Cooking takes about 25 minutes.

Freezing: Freeze the pancakes, well wrapped, for up to 6 months. Allow to defrost before using.

Carob Sundae

A delightful treat which provides the perfect end to any meal.

SERVES 4

Carob dessert

225ml/8 fl oz milk or soya milk
1 tsp vanilla essence
1 tbsp sunflower oil
2 tbsps honey
¼ tsp salt
1 tbsp cornflour
¼ tsp Caro (coffee substitute)
1 tbsp carob powder

Vanilla custard

1 tbsp cornflour
120ml/4fl oz milk or soya milk
1 tbsp honey
½ tsp vanilla essence

Filling

1 large banana, chopped
1 punnet of strawberries, hulled, washed and halved

Blend all the carob dessert ingredients in a saucepan and cook until thick, stirring continuously. Leave to cool. Mix the cornflour with a little of the milk to make a smooth paste and add the honey and vanilla essence. Heat the remaining milk until nearly boiling and pour over the cornflour mixture, stirring until smooth. Return to the pan and re-heat gently until thick, stirring constantly. Leave to cool. Add half the carob dessert to the chopped banana and mix together carefully. Fill sundae glasses with layers of carob dessert, banana mixture, strawberries, vanilla custard and finally the plain carob dessert.

Chill before serving.

Time: Preparation takes 20 minutes,
cooking takes 10 minutes.

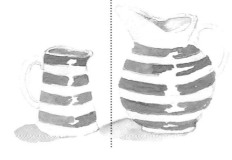

Halva of Carrots & Cashews

Halva is a traditional Indian dessert made from carrots and cream. Do not let the use of vegetables in a dessert put you off trying this rather special recipe, as the results are really delicious.

SERVES 4-6

900g/2lbs carrots, peeled
280ml/¹/₂ pint double cream
175g/6oz dark muscovado sugar
2 tbsps clear honey
2 tsps ground coriander
1 tsp ground cinnamon
Pinch of saffron
60g/2oz butter or margarine
60g/2oz raisins
120g/4oz unsalted cashew nuts, chopped
Candied violets, silver balls or desiccated coconut, to decorate

Grate the carrots using the coarse side of a grater. Place the carrot, cream, sugar, honey and spices in a large saucepan. Mix well. Cook over a low heat for 15-20 minutes until the carrots are soft, stirring frequently during the cooking to prevent burning.

Add the butter or margarine, raisins and nuts, stir well and continue cooking for 10-15 minutes until the mixture has thickened and the carrots are well broken down. Pile into serving dishes and decorate with candied violets, silver balls or coconut. Time: Preparation takes about 15 minutes, cooking takes about 30 minutes.

Chocolate Orange Cheesecake

Chocolate and orange, a favourite combination for many, are combined in this delicious, rich cheesecake.

SERVES 8-10

90g/3oz butter or margarine, melted
175g/6oz chocolate digestive biscuits, crushed
450g/1lb full-fat cream cheese
120g/4oz caster sugar
Grated rind and juice of 1 orange
280ml/¹/₂ pint Greek-style yogurt
1 tbsp agar-agar
3 tbsps water
60g/2oz plain chocolate, melted
2 oranges, peeled and segmented

Mix together the butter or margarine and biscuits and press into the bottom of a 20.5cm/8-inch loose-bottomed cake tin. Chill. Beat together the cream cheese and sugar and then beat in the orange juice and rind. Fold in the yogurt. Sprinkle the agar-agar over the water. Set over hot water until dissolved then stir into the cream cheese mixture.

Pile the cheese mixture on top of the biscuit base, and level the top. Drizzle about two-thirds of the melted chocolate over the top and swirl a skewer through the mixture to create a marbled effect. Chill until set. Transfer to a serving dish and arrange the orange segments on top. Decorate with the remaining chocolate. Time: Preparation takes about 30 minutes, plus chilling.

Cranberry Fool

A simple and refreshing dessert.

SERVES 4

225g/8oz fresh cranberries
2 tbsps clear honey
90g/3oz whipping cream
120g/4oz Greek yogurt
Toasted flaked almonds

Rinse the cranberries and stew with a scant amount of water until softened. Remove from the heat, add the honey and leave to cool. Whip the cream and gently fold in the yogurt. Combine the yogurt and cream with the cooled cranberries. Divide the mixture between four stem glasses and decorate with toasted flaked almonds.
Time: Preparation takes 10 minutes, cooking takes 15-20 minutes.
Variation: As fresh cranberries may be available only at Christmas time, redcurrants would make an excellent summer substitute.

Apricot Fool

Serve this dessert in individual serving glasses and decorate with curls of chocolate or carob.

SERVES 4

225g/8oz dried apricots
1 ripe banana
1 small carton natural strained yogurt
1 egg
Few squares carob chocolate

Soak the apricots in water for at least 1 hour. Cook until soft then purée. Mash the banana and add to the apricot purée. Fold the yogurt into the fruit mixture. Separate the egg and stir the yolk into fruit mixture. Whisk the egg white until stiff then fold into the fruit mixture.
Time: Preparation takes 10 minutes. Soaking and cooking takes about 2 hours 40 minutes.
Variation: Decorate with toasted almonds.

Plum & Ginger Crisp

Plums and ginger biscuits complement each other beautifully in this simple dish.

SERVES 4-6

450g/1lb dessert plums
60g/2oz light muscovado sugar
3 tbsps orange juice
75g/2½ oz unsalted butter or margarine
225g/8oz ginger biscuits, crushed
60g/2oz flaked almonds

Wash and halve the plums and remove the stones. Place the plums, sugar and orange juice in a pie dish. Melt the butter or margarine and stir in the crushed biscuits and almonds. Mix well to coat all the crumbs. Sprinkle the biscuit topping over the fruit and level the top. Bake in an oven preheated to 180°C/ 350°F/Gas Mark 4, for 25 minutes. Cover with foil if the topping begins to brown too much.

Time: Preparation takes about 15 minutes, cooking takes about 25 minutes.

Variation: Use apricots instead of the plums and wholemeal digestive biscuits instead of the ginger biscuits.

Strawberry Sorbet

Serve at the end of a very rich meal or between the main course and dessert if serving a light summer dinner.

SERVES 4

1 medium lemon
280ml/½ pint water
175g/6oz sugar
680g/1½lbs strawberries
2 egg whites

Pare the rind from the lemon and put into the water with the sugar. Heat slowly until the sugar has dissolved then boil for 5 minutes. Strain and set aside to cool. Hull the strawberries, reserving a few for decoration. Press the remainder through a nylon sieve and add the juice of half the lemon. Whisk the egg whites until very stiff. Combine all the ingredients well. Put into an airtight container and place in the freezer. Remove when half frozen, beat well and return to the freezer. Place in the refrigerator about 1 hour before serving. Serve in wine glasses topped with the whole berries.

Time: Preparation takes 20 minutes, cooking takes 5 minutes. Freezing takes about 8 hours.

Cook's Tip: It is better to leave the sorbet in the freezer overnight after beating.

Poached Pears with Raspberry Coulis

This simple-to-prepare dessert is superb when lightly perfumed with the fragrance of fresh hyssop, but you can use cinnamon instead.

SERVES 4

280ml/½ pint water

60ml/4 tbsps clear honey

1 tbsp lemon juice

2 sprigs fresh hyssop or 1 stick cinnamon

4 pears with stalks

225g/8oz raspberries

1 tsp chopped fresh hyssop to decorate (optional)

Place the water and honey in a large saucepan or frying pan and heat until honey dissolves. Stir in the lemon juice and hyssop or cinnamon stick. Peel the pears and carefully cut them in half lengthways with a sharp knife, splitting the stalk if possible. Keep the stalks intact if possible, and remove the core with a grapefruit knife or teaspoon. Put the pears in the syrup and bring gently to the boil. Cover, reduce the heat, and simmer gently until the pears are tender. Chill until required.

Meanwhile, purée the raspberries and chopped hyssop in a food processor or liquidiser and push through a sieve to remove the seeds. Sweeten the raspberry coulis with a little of the honey syrup if wished. Arrange the pears on serving plates and pour a little raspberry coulis over each. Decorate with sprigs of hyssop, if wished, and serve the remaining sauce separately.

Time: Preparation takes about 20 minutes, plus chilling. Cooking takes about 10 minutes.

Baked Bananas with Sauce à la Poire

Baked bananas are an established favourite and served with this delightful fruity sauce they are particularly delicious.

SERVES 4

2 small oranges

2 ripe pears, peeled and cored

Honey to taste

4 bananas

Using a potato peeler, pare the rind from one of the oranges, taking care not to include too much white pith. Cut the pared rind into very thin strips with a sharp knife and blanch in boiling water for 2-3 minutes, to soften. Drain and set aside. Cut off all the remaining peel and pith from the orange using a sharp knife, then carefully cut out the orange segments from in between the membranes. Squeeze the juice from the other orange. Place the orange juice and pears in a food processor and purée until smooth. Sweeten to taste with honey.

Peel the bananas, place in an ovenproof dish and pour the pear purée over the top. Cover, and bake in a preheated oven at 180°C/350°F/Gas Mark 4 for 15 minutes or until the pears are soft. Decorate with the orange segments and strips of orange rind. Serve immediately.

Time: Preparation takes about 10 minutes, cooking takes is about 15 minutes.

Preparation: This dessert is best prepared as late as possible to prevent discolouration of the fruit.

Index